BRIT GUIDE

Brilliant Days at
DISNEYLAND
PARIS

BRIT GUIDE RESEARCH TEAM

D1334165

LO

W.Foulsham & Co. Ltd

For Foulsham Publishing Ltd
The Old Barrel Store
Drayman's Lane
Marlow
Bucks SL7 2FF

Foulsham books can be found in all good bookshops and direct from www.foulsham.com

ISBN: 978-0-572-04699-6
Copyright © 2017 W. Foulsham & Co. Ltd.

The moral rights of the authors have been asserted
CIP record for this book is available from the British Library

Photograph acknowledgements
Cover: **Hipark Serris Val d'Europe** (top left), **Joe Jukes** (top middle two), **Chris Brewer** (top right), **Joe Jukes** (all bottom row)
Chris Brewer 116 (bottom)
Domaine de Crécy 37
Eddie Nock 85
Eric De Maertelaere 4, 5, 8, 93, 97 (top), 107, 108–9, 121 (bottom), 128–9, 142 (bottom)
Eurostar 20
Hilary White 65, 68–9, 88, 90 (top)
Hipark Serris Val d'Europe 31
Hotel l'Elysée Val d'Europe 30
Joe Jukes 7, 16, 21, 45, 49, 56–7, 60, 74, 75, 77, 78, 80, 81, 82, 84, 86, 87, 89, 90 (bottom), 91, 92, 95, 96, 97 (middle and bottom), 98, 100, 101, 102, 104, 110, 114, 115, 116 (top), 117, 118, 119, 120, 121 (top), 122, 123, 124, 125, 130, 132–3, 135, 138, 139, 140, 141, 142 (top), 143, 144
M Hotson 59, 94, 148
Sealife Aquarium 149
Vienna House Dream Castle Hotel 29
Vienna House Magic Circus Hotel 33

Contents

Introduction

With over 14 million visitors passing through its gates every year, Disneyland Paris has become one of Europe's most popular holiday destinations and for good reason – you don't have to be a child or have children with you to enjoy the fun.

Main Street USA

Families, groups, couples and singles from all over the world have not only opted to visit this resort on holiday, but many have returned time and time again to both relive the magic and experience something new from its many attractions.

Having opened its gates for the first time to the public on 12 April 1992, 2017 marked the resort's **25th Anniversary** and, in true Disney style, both parks showcased a range of magnificent and inspiring celebrations for all of its guests.

If you have visited Disneyland Paris before you will notice the improvements to the overall décor and appearance of both parks which are the result of the two-year 'Experience Enhancement Program' (EEP). Classic attractions including but not limited to **Peter Pan's Flight**, **Big Thunder Mountain** and **it's a small world** have benefitted hugely not just from a lick of paint but from thorough renovations which added new scenes to the experience and detail in the design. A tidy-up of everything outside in the parks, from the paving slabs to the gardens to the Castle fascia has made the parks feel fresh and new again.

Alongside the EEP, comes the brand new launch of **Star Tours: The Adventure Continues** – a complete renovation and reworking of the old Star Tours motion simulator ride to bring it up to date with the movie franchise; and, to further tie in with Disney's acquisition of *Star Wars* from Lucasfilm in 2012, the transformation of **Space Mountain: Mission 2** into **Star Wars Hyperspace Mountain**. This last innovation has been the subject of much concern and consternation on the Disneyland Paris fansites, with dedicated followers bewailing the fate of this much-loved and admired Paris ride as it is transformed from its original Jules Verne-inspired theme into 'yet another' *Star Wars* attraction. How the new ride ultimately fares only time will tell, but it is certainly true that for the new generation of children and for those yet to come, *Star Wars* holds an enduring fascination and popularity.

When it comes to big anniversaries, Disney are not usually shy about prolonging their celebrations for as long as possible so it is likely that the special 25th anniversary events will continue to run throughout 2018. With more to see and do than ever, and the parks glittering from their fresh revamps, there couldn't be a better time to make your first trip through the front gates of Disneyland Park, down Main Street USA, and up to the iconic Sleeping Beauty Castle.

> *"You can design and create, and build the most wonderful place in the world. But it takes people to make the dream a reality."*
>
> Walt Disney

What can you find at Disneyland Paris?

Before you can make the decision to book your tickets, you will want to know what adventures are in store for you and your family at this unique resort.

Disneyland Paris is split into two separate theme parks that sit side-by-side in an area to the East of Paris called **Marne-la-Vallée**. The first is **Disneyland Park**, and the second, smaller, area is **Walt Disney Studios**.

Disneyland Park

With the iconic Sleeping Beauty Castle forming its centrepiece, Disneyland Park is divided seamlessly into five lands to explore.

Step through the front gates on to the busy boulevard of boutiques that forms **Main Street USA** before you reach the central roundabout. From here you can wander into the Wild West of **Frontierland** or the futuristic space-themed **Discoveryland**, where you can find popular rides such as **Star Wars Hyperspace Mountain** and **Star Tours**. Head for **Adventureland** and you will discover a dangerous tropical world of pirates and foreign lands or step into

5

Fantasyland, a dream-world of princesses, flying elephants, dragons and fairy tales.

Walt Disney Studios

Walt Disney Studios turns its visitors' attention away from the on-screen action to provide a behind-the-scenes – and beyond the camera lens – tour of the Disney magic. As guests enter the Front Lot through the gates, they immediately find themselves on film set after elaborate film set, or watching live action shows of their favourite Disney characters.

With its four unique Hollywood-inspired zones – the **Front Lot**, the **Toon Studio**, the **Backlot** and the **Production Courtyard** – visitors can become the star of their very own blockbuster. Pixar animation comes to life before your very eyes on the popular *Finding Nemo*-based **Crush's Coaster**; in **Toy Story Playland**; and in the newest addition to the park: **Ratatouille: The Adventure**. For the thrill-seekers in your family, the **Twilight Zone Tower of Terror** rises up into the skyline of the Studios for those who dare to test its haunted elevator, while the **Rock 'n' Roller Coaster Starring Aerosmith** literally blasts riders off on a high-speed whirl of loops, twists and turns – not for the faint-hearted!

Shows and Parades

Take a seat for the countless live action and animated shows available across the parks throughout the year, where Jedis, princesses and those classic characters Mickey Mouse and Donald Duck come to life before your very eyes. **Disney Stars on Parade** takes place every day in the Disneyland Park and every night the sky is lit up with the lights and music of **Disney Illuminations**, which closes every day at Disneyland Paris with a happy ending.

See chapters five to seven for everything you need to know about the two parks: attractions, shows, parades and dining.

The Disney Village

Just to the right of the Disney Studios, and directly opposite Disneyland Park, you will find all of your food, entertainment and merchandise needs catered for in Disney Village. With toy, Lego and clothes stores, and restaurants ranging from McDonalds to Planet Hollywood to the classic American steakhouse, the Village has a little something for everyone.

Disney Village also offers ample entertainment in the form of IMAX cinemas and music and live-action arena performances with Billy Bob's Country and Western Saloon and Buffalo Bill's Wild West Show.

Chapter eight provides an in-depth look at everything this bustling lakeside community has on offer.

The Disneyland Hotel.

Hotels

With 14 million guests visiting the Marne-la-Vallée region each year for the parks alone, hundreds of hotels have opened to accommodate them. Disneyland has a selection of its own expertly themed and luxuriously decorated hotels to choose from, whether you are looking to stay in the 5-star Victorian mansion that is the **Disneyland Hotel**, or one of the cosy woodland lodges at the **Davy Crockett Ranch**.

The Walt Disney Co. have also selected a group of eight different **Partner Hotels** that lie in the region. These also provide a little something for everyone, whether it's a spa or sauna to return to after a hectic day in the theme parks, or a game or two of golf.

See chapter three for descriptions of many Disney, Partner and other hotel options with price comparisons.

Dining

From a quick fix snack to elegant fine cuisine, the choice of restaurants across both of the parks and throughout the hotels is exhaustive. The eateries stretch from simple one-stop sandwich shops – such as the New York Style Sandwiches shop in the Disney Village – to the table service and menu à *la Française* at Chez Remy. Each Disney Hotel offers its own unique dining experience with a mixture of table and buffet service options, alongside multiple themed and elegant bars for you to while away a relaxed evening with a cocktail of your choice.

To help in your selection process, we have included TripAdvisor ratings and direct quotes from countless reviews for most of the dining options throughout the book.

Meeting the characters

Have you or your children ever wanted to meet a real life Disney character? Book a character meal at either **Auberge de Cendrillon**, **Inventions** at the Disneyland Hotel or **Plaza Gardens Restaurant** (breakfast only) and make your dreams come true as they meet their on-screen heroes and heroines. If you aren't able to splash out on one of the dining opportunities (and these are pricey), Disney characters make appearances in designated areas and at fixed meet-and-greet venues throughout both parks, as well as in the lobbies of most of the Disney Hotels each morning, to meet their fans and pose for a picture. No one needs to leave their stay at Disneyland Paris without having some time up-close and personal with a character or two.

Golf

Not only does Disneyland Paris provide its own 18-hole golf course nearby, but also Marne-la-Vallée holds excellent alternative options for the avid or budding golfer. Check out our detailed section in chapter nine to see our breakdown of the prices alongside a small list of those hotels closest to the green.

Shops

From collectible prints, to hundreds of plush toys, there is a shop or boutique to suit every Disney-merchandise need throughout Disneyland Paris. There are also two shopping centres a short distance by RER train from the parks: Val d'Europe and La Vallée.

The Disney Store in Disney Village.

How long do I need?

The Disneyland Paris website recommends its guests stay for three to four days to get the most out of this unique and magical experience and most packages offer two- three- and four-night stays. Certainly, it's advisable for first-time visitors to go for the maximum time they can afford. You will need to allow at least two full days to do the Disneyland Park comfortably and a day for Walt Disney Studios. Even then, you are unlikely to be able to do it all in this time, especially at peak times and if you have younger children.

Planning your trip

So now that you know a bit about what's on offer it's time to think about planning your trip.

Booking the various elements of your holiday well in advance – including hotel, travel tickets or park tickets – will save you lots of money.

If you venture on to the Disneyland Paris website, you will find that it is very easy to book a simple and all-inclusive package deal that fulfils your holiday requirements for accommodation, park tickets and dining. However, there are countless other choices available to you outside of these package deals that allow you to tailor your holiday to the limits of your budget and to suit you and your family's requirements.

The next four chapters are designed to help you sift through these choices and to make those all-important decisions about when to go, how to get there, where to stay and which tickets to buy. We compare prices, show you how to get the best deals and offer some tips along the way.

Using this guide

There isn't always room in a book to provide all the information you need and some information quickly goes out of date. We've included QR codes throughout this guide to give you direct access to unique online material. This includes travel and hotel cost comparisons, itineraries for different age groups at the parks and interactive theme park maps.

To access this information on your smartphone you'll need a built-in camera and a QR code reader app which you can normally download for free from the App Store, Google Play, Blackberry World or your relevant app store. Just search for 'QR code reader' or 'QR code scanner'. Once you've downloaded your preferred app, open it up and select the scanning option which should turn on your phone's camera.

Scan the QR code above for the Disneyland Paris website.

1 When to go

One of the best things about Disneyland Paris is that there isn't one perfect time of year to visit. Whether you want to avoid the crowds, are tied to school holidays, are looking for budget options or want to visit for a special occasion, whatever month suits you you will find plenty to enjoy. Here are a few things to consider in your planning.

Getting the best deals

Disneyland Paris divides its year into six different cost categories:

- **Super Value** around January 8–February 2nd
- **Value** February to late March and most of November
- **Moderate** From April to May and most of September
- **Regular** June plus weekends throughout the year
- **High** July
- **Peak** August, October 22–31 (Halloween), December 22–31 and 1-7 January (Christmas and New Year)

Scan the QR code above for the Disneyland Paris online brochures.

The full range of dates that these categories cover can be found in both the Disneyland Paris catalogue and their detailed price guide, both of which can be found by scanning the QR code on this page.

While the price of park tickets doesn't vary excessively, the Disney Hotels and the Partner Hotels base their pricing on these designated periods – so watch out! These prices are covered in more detail in Chapter 4.

Special seasonal offers

There are also seasonal offers to keep your eye out for that could save you money if you are willing and able to travel to the parks during those off-peak times of the year. Take a look at the offers currently available through the links in our 'Which Tickets to Buy' section on pages 44–45.

Climate

The climate in Paris, being northern Europe, is similar to the UK although it is usually noticeably warmer during the summer than at home. A good week in August in Paris is much more likely to hit the 30°+ mark than in London. Heavy summer showers and indeed rainfall throughout the year are to be expected but, fortunately, Disneyland Paris was designed with the Parisian climate in mind so there is plenty of shelter throughout the parks, and many indoor rides.

Through the seasons

Winter

If you don't mind fighting the cold and rain, then visiting during the winter season (excluding Christmas) is definitely a money-saving option. Hotel rooms are substantially cheaper during January and February and park tickets usually feature excellent deals during this period in an attempt to draw in the crowds. There are sometimes packages available which include a free Disney Dining Plan (see page 54), which could save you a lot of money on park restaurant food during your holiday. Queues for attractions, even the most popular ones, are far shorter, sometimes non-existent, saving you and your family the hours you will spend queuing during the summer. A major downside of a winter visit, though, is the regular ride closures. Winter is naturally the prime time for Disney to carry out any necessary repairs and refurbishments on some of its most popular rides, so you can expect this to affect you to some degree during these months. It is possible to check online which closures are in operation, although often not very far in advance.

The Christmas and New Year period is a wonderful time to visit the parks but, of course, at this time you lose the quiet, queue-free atmosphere – and the attractive prices too. The Christmas season, which runs from November to early January, is very popular in the parks and really brings in the crowds, although visiting in November or early December before the schools have broken up will obviously be a little quieter than the Christmas period itself. Everywhere you look you will see the glittering festive decorations and seasonal theming (see pages 14–17), and you can even book into one of the Christmas-themed rooms at the Disney Hotels. Check the Disneyland Paris website for price details.

Spring

Spring still brings those snaps of cold and with it the potential for rain, but there are so many covered shows, rides and

BRIT TIP

The queues for outdoor rides may be shorter when it rains if you are happy to brave it – although don't always bank on this. In summer if it's warm and wet you can expect plenty of people to have the same idea, sadly.

activities in Disneyland Paris that showers aren't too much of a problem. Prices during this time are a little bit higher than winter, especially during the school holidays and festivals such as Easter and any other spring celebrations.

Summer

Summer is the natural peak in the year for the parks' popularity, combining the school holidays with a good dose of much-needed sunshine and warm weather around the Paris region. Of course you are looking at peak-time prices within the resort itself, although you can find some excellent deals at many of the other surrounding hotels in the Marne-la-Vallée region. Take a look at our Hotel Comparison Tables on pages 26–27 for more details.

Summertime at Disneyland Paris brings with it crowds of families and students to the parks and the hotel pools, and it's no surprise that the queues for the popular rides and for certain high-demand restaurants are dramatically increased.

A big benefit of visiting in the school summer holidays is the extended park opening hours, with the Disneyland Park open every night until 11pm. The final spectacle of the day is the Disney Illuminations light, special effects and fireworks show. Some areas of the park will close 1–2 hours before the show to allow for setting up, but unlike in many UK theme parks, the majority of the rides and attractions outside of those areas will stay open until the end. This means that if you've already seen the show, you can benefit from some short queues on some of the other popular rides late in the evening. Make a note, though, that if this idea appeals but you plan to go at the very end of August or into the first few days of September, check which date the extended opening hours end, as the French school holiday season tends to finish a week or so before that in the UK. If this information is not available when you book, a look back at the previous year's pattern might be helpful.

Autumn

It's no surprise that the Halloween period and autumn school half term is the busiest time in the resort during autumn. Celebrating Halloween at Disneyland Paris promises to be a dark and delightful treat for all ages (see page 14), with an annual night-time party in Disneyland Park costing around €45 per person. Outside of this, autumn offers the same relative peace and quiet as spring, although with the same caveat regarding inclement weather. On the whole though, if you are not tied to the school timetable it's a good time to consider.

Calendar of seasonal events

The following events, shows and entertainment usually take place each year. Use the QR code to view the information on your smartphone for exact timings and dates for 2018. Prices correct at time of writing but subject to annual increase so check on the Disneyland Paris website before booking.

January–March
Children under 12 go free during this quieter season.

Early March
St David's Welsh Festival
Events take place at Disney Village and Disneyland Park for this mini festival featuring Disney characters dressed up in Welsh costume, live bands and a traditional Welsh choir. There is also a crafts market, traditional food and drink, face painting and a special fireworks display.

16 March
Birthday of Walt Disney Studios
See park guide on the day for details.

17 March
St Patrick's Day
Events for St Patrick's Day consist of live traditional music, characters dressed in Irish costume, a pre-parade with green floats and Irish dancers and a special Irish-themed fireworks display in the evening.

12 April
Birthday of Disneyland Paris
See park guide on the day for details.

14 July
Bastille Day
There is a special extra fireworks display in the evening before the main fireworks to celebrate this French National Day.

Mid-September
Disneyland Paris Half-Marathon Weekend
In the main half-marathon (13.1 miles) event participants run through both Disney theme parks, Disney Village and local villages. Characters are positioned along the route and there is a medal for all those who finish the race. Other events across the weekend include a 5K and 10K race, and *run* Disney Kids races. In previous years, all the race-only places have sold out on the release day in January.

Scan the QR code above for more information on timings and dates for 2018.

October to early November
Disney's Halloween Festival

Disney's Halloween Festival has become nearly as popular as Christmas and you can expect a high volume of crowds during this season which runs throughout October.

The parks are extravagantly themed and decorated throughout with bright autumn colours, Mickey-shaped pumpkins and some spooky surprises. Disney characters are dressed in Halloween-themed costumes and you can buy villain-style merchandise, have your face painted or even choose a Halloween option from the menu in some restaurants.

Meet-and-greets also take on the Halloween theming. Mickey can be found all dressed up in Cottonwood Creek Ranch, Frontierland, and Goofy in Town Square with his trick or treat candy machine. Head to Casey Corner on Main Street USA to meet Stitch and Minnie at their Costume Couture, or Frontierland for a photo opportunity with Jack and Sally from *Nightmare Before Christmas* at their specially created cemetery. Maleficent greets guests in the courtyard area at the back of Sleeping Beauty Castle.

Certain Disney film villains take part in a short musical presentation at the Castle Stage in front of the castle and are available afterwards for meet and greets.

Mickey and Minnie, Huey, Louis and Dewy, Scrooge Mc Duck, Clarabelle Cow and others celebrate the rich colours of autumn and abundance of harvest at Mickey's Halloween Cavalcade Celebration. This mini-parade follows the main parade route and takes place three times a day.

Disney villains try to take over the show at the special Halloween-themed version of Disney Illuminations.

The Halloween Party is a separate ticketed event costing €45 per person that takes place in Disney Village from 8.30pm–1am on 31 Oct. Most park attractions will be open during the event and there is additional live entertainment. Guests may dress up in Halloween costume with certain stipulations.

Early November
Mickey's Magical Fireworks and Bonfire

A 3-night special for Bonfire Night with evening fireworks and special effects shows on and above Lake Disney.

Mid-November to early January
Disney's Enchanted Christmas

Christmas is the biggest entertainment programme of the

year and is one of the most magical times to visit with festive decorations, snow effects, a sparkling castle, unique gifts and seasonal shows, parades and fireworks. This is a broad overview of what you can expect to find, but use our QR code on page 13 to check for the latest information.

Disneyland Park

Main Street USA is transformed into a winter wonderland with festoons, lights and snowfall five times a day.

Santa rides his toy-laden sleigh down Fantasyland and Main Street USA in true Disney style at the special Christmas Parade. This cheerful musical procession includes all your favourite Disney characters in festive finery, various performers and fantastic Christmas-themed floats. The parade takes place three times a day for the whole season although Santa will only take part up until 25th December. This is in addition to the regular Disney Stars on Parade.

Well-loved princes and princesses take to the dance floor for Royal Christmas Wishes, a dazzling show at the Royal Castle Stage.

Guests can join Anna and Elsa at the Arendelle winter festival for a wintry-style *Frozen* Sing-Along, featuring many of the best songs from the film. This well-produced show is performed six times a day in the week and 12 times a day on weekends and peak days at the Chaparral Theatre. The sisters also ride through the park in their horse-drawn carriage three times a day.

For a memorable moment with Santa, and a classic photo opportunity, head for the Cottonwood Creek Ranch where he has his own special chalet. Mickey will also be there along with Merida (the princess from *Brave*) and Jack from *Nightmare before Christmas*. Miss Bunny and Thumper can be found at Casey's Corner.

In the evening guests can gather at Town Square in front of the 40ft Christmas tree and watch it come to life with the help of Mickey, Minnie and Santa at Mickey's Magical Christmas Lights. This show takes place twice daily.

Disney Illuminations at Christmas is a seasonal version of the regular night-time show. Characters from Disney classics are projected on to the front of the castle and you can expect all the favourite characters to take the lead in the show. There are also scenes of Christmas from across the world. It is accompanied by several songs from *Frozen*, fireworks, water fountains and special effects.

New Year's Eve fireworks.

Walt Disney Studios

Enter Studio 1 and you will be greeted in true Hollywood style by big band Christmas music. Outside, the entrance courtyard is tastefully decorated with Christmas trees, tinsel, decorations and lights and is the place to meet Mickey Mouse each morning and afternoon. Don't forget to look out for the snow shower at the Umbrellas of Cherbourg in Backlot, too.

Disney Village

There are Christmas decorations throughout Disney Village and you can sample some traditional festive food such as pain d'épices, roasted chestnuts and mulled wine. At Buffalo Bill's Wild West Show you can enjoy a Christmas and New Year version of the menu priced at around £89–105 for adults, and £48–56 for 3–11s.

Hotels and dining

Each resort hotel has a beautifully decorated Christmas tree in the lobby area to get you into the Christmas spirit. In addition to its tree, Disneyland Hotel also has a huge Gingerbread House made with real gingerbread pieces while Hotel New York has an ice-skating rink.

Some hotels offer special meals over the Christmas period but these come with a hefty price tag. The Christmas Eve Dinners (no characters) in several hotels, Disney Village and Disneyland Park cost between £80–243 for adults and £24–£56 for 3–11s. Hotel New York and Auberge du Cendrillon offer these with characters which bumps the price up to £178–£194 per adults and £56 per child.

On Christmas Day there is a 4-course Merry Christmas Lunch with Goofy and Santa Claus at the Hotel New York for £121 per adult and £48 per child.

31 December
New Year's Eve

This is traditionally the busiest day at the resort: crowds will be at their optimum level and you can expect long wait times for rides. However, the special fireworks display is a great way to see the New Year in and guests can stick around afterwards as the parks stay open until 1am. There are also a number of exclusive dining options for New Year's Eve including a character buffet at Hotel New York and full service dinner at Auberge de Cendrillon ranging from £186–£235 per adult and £56–£64 per child. Regular dinners are served at the hotels, Billy Bob's Saloon and The Steakhouse in Disney Village and at Disneyland park restaurants ranging from £97–£292 per adult and £32–£72 per child. All seasonal prices correct at time of writing but subject to annual increase.

Your own special occasions

You may want to visit Disneyland Paris to coincide with your own special occasion such as a birthday or anniversary. Let them know at City Hall or Studio Services that it's your birthday and you will be given a 'Happy Birthday' sticker to wear throughout the day. If it's a little one's birthday ask a Cast Member if one of the characters has a special message and you will be taken to a room where the phone rings and a recorded message wishes them 'Happy Birthday'.

All table service and buffet restaurants can supply a birthday cake or special dessert for €31. Simply order it when you make your dining reservation or at your hotel information desk, at the restaurant front desk, city hall or studio services.

Avoiding the busiest times

Public holidays are always more crowded at the parks so if you want to avoid this, don't visit on the following dates:

- 1 Jan
- Easter Monday
- 1 May
- 8 May
- Ascension Day
- Whit Monday
- 14 July
- 15 August
- 1 November
- 11 November
- Christmas Day

2 **Getting there**

Despite its name, Disneyland Paris is not actually inside the French capital, but is instead a short train ride or drive out of the city towards the East in the Marne-la-Vallée region.

There are so many different travel options available to take you directly to Disneyland Paris, whether you decide to travel independently by car, or if you think the special Disney Eurostar provides the magical experience you are looking for.

By car

If you are travelling from the UK, one of the cheapest and simplest ways of getting there is by car. You have the option of taking the ferry or Eurotunnel to cross the channel.

P&O Ferries from Dover to Calais
- The crossing takes about 90 minutes
- There are around 20 crossings per day
- There are shops, restaurants and bars on board to provide you with entertainment
- Disneyland Paris is only a three hour drive from Calais
- Standard flexi tickets start at £55 each way per car

To take a look at the times and prices of the P&O Ferry crossings, scan the QR code to visit their website.

The Eurotunnel from Folkestone to Calais
- The crossing takes around 35 minutes
- There are a maximum of four shuttles per hour
- Disneyland Paris is only a three hour drive from Calais
- Short stay saver tickets start at £58 each way per car

Scan the QR code to learn more about the times and prices of the Eurotunnel service.

Directions from Calais to Disneyland Paris
- Take the A26 from Calais
- Change on to the A4
- Continue to follow the A4 or the A104: it will take you straight to the parks
- Disneyland will be well signposted along the way

Scan the QR code above for the P&O Ferries website.

Scan the QR code above for the Eurotunnel website.

Parking at Disneyland Paris

- For guests of the Disney hotels, parking at both their hotel and the parks is free
- Check whether you can park for free at the parks if you stay at any of the other hotels – it's not always a standard feature
- Parking is free for Annual Pass holders

Prices at the Disney Car Park in front of the parks

- Cars cost €20 per day
- Vehicles over 2 metres high cost €20 per day
- Campervans cost €35 per day
- Motorbikes cost €15 per day

Hints for driving in France

- Don't rely solely on a satnav. There is a danger they can lead you astray, and they are sometimes distracting. By all means have it alongside, but always use a map and plan your route in advance.
- Any type of device that alerts you to speed cameras (including those built into satnavs) is illegal in France.
- It is illegal for children under 10 to travel in the front seat.
- Speed limit signage can be poor so check this out in advance so you are not relying on looking for signs.
- Speed limits can vary in wet weather on the motorways.
- Hypermarket petrol stations usually offer the best prices. The closest hypermarket to Disneyland Paris is Carrefour Bailly Romainvilliers. The closest actual petrol station is situated near the Hotel Santa Fe, close to the exit from the Disney car park, but prices will be higher here.
- Alcohol limits are lower than the UK and the penalties for being over the limit are very high. Don't take the risk of trying to calculate a 'safe' amount – stick to the coffee if you are driving.
- It is now illegal to drive a car greater than 20 years old in Paris.
- By law, to drive in Paris you must now display a sticker in the window of your car giving the vehicle's emissions. These stickers are only available from the French government website certificat-air.gouv.fr, there is a small charge and they will take up to six weeks to arrive by post.
- The AA's guide to driving in France is excellent for information on French motoring rules and regulations and for a list of the essential items you must have in your car by law. Scan the QR code to check this out.

Scan the QR code above for our travel cost comparison.

Scan the QR code above for the AA's guide to driving in France.

By Eurostar or rail services

Eurostar from London to Disneyland Paris

During certain popular times of the year, such as school holidays and weekends, there is a Eurostar direct service straight to Disneyland Paris. This is a great option as it avoids the hassle and extra time involved in arriving at Gare du Nord in the centre of Paris and transferring on to Marne-la-Vallee.

Eurostar.

Take the Eurostar from London St Pancras, Ashford or Ebbsfleet and in 2 hours and 40 minutes you will arrive at the Marne-la-Vallée/Chessy station, which is situated right outside the entrance to the parks and the Disney Village. Fares direct to Disneyland from the UK (London St. Pancras, Ashford International and Ebbsfleet International) start from £38 one-way for adults and £27 one-way for children aged between 4 and 11, based on a return journey. Children under 4 travel for free.

 Scan the QR code above for the Eurostar website.

Tickets and booking on the Eurostar is more akin to flight tickets and airline procedure than to British Network rail trains. You cannot stand on the train – every passenger must be in an allocated seat, with the exception of under 4s who can sit on an adult's lap. Ticket sales open 6 months in advance so best to book as early as possible to access the best fares and availability.

If you are booking through Disney you have the option to include your Eurostar tickets in your package. This is the easiest option as you can add on Disney Express at the point of booking (see below) and you are guaranteed to secure your train tickets along with the rest of your package. However, it is still worth checking the price Disney are charging against the price on the Eurostar website. It is sometimes (although not always) much cheaper to book your travel separately.

If you do want to book your Eurostar tickets separately from the rest of your package, make absolutely certain that there are suitable seats available on the required train before you book your hotel package and book them as soon as – or even immediately before – you book your holiday.

BRIT TIP ☑

Disney block-book a huge number of seats on the direct Eurostar service for their customers, so DO NOT assume that you can easily book seats at any time before you travel. There is often very limited availability on the service.

Disney Express Luggage Service

Alongside your Disney hotel and park tickets package, you have the option to add on the Disney Express luggage service. This provides a number of convenient transfer options, some before you have even set foot in France:

- If you booked Disney Express along with your package and are on the direct train, a Disney Cast member will pass through the train to check you into your hotel and give you your park tickets. When you get off the train, find your way to the Disney Express counter to drop off your luggage and then you are free to head straight into the parks.
- If you booked Disney Express along with your package but are on an indirect train; if you booked it through one of Disney's preferred travel agents; or if you added it to your package through the call centre (see below), at Marne-la-Vallee/Chessy station find your way to the Disney Express counter to pick up your park tickets and advance check-in documents and drop off your bags.
- Your luggage is transferred to your Disney or Partner Hotel for you.
- Your luggage will also be transferred directly to the station for you when you check out of your hotel.

This service is no longer added as a free perk for people booking their travel through Disney and is charged at a standard €17 per person for everyone over the age of 3. If you're booking your rail travel independently, you can add Disney Express to your hotel package by calling the Disneyland Paris call centre on 08448 008 898, quoting your hotel booking details and requesting to add it on for the additional charge.

Disney Express is not available for anyone staying outside of the Disney and Partner Hotels.

Weigh up the pros and cons of Disney Express for yourself before you book it. If you're travelling in a group €17 per person will add up. If you're staying for a reasonably long break, you might prefer to take your time checking in to your hotel and getting your bearings. Some members of your party might welcome the chance to freshen up after the journey, or stop for a drink in the hotel bar on arrival. When it comes to your departure, if you travel light and don't have too much luggage, you might prefer to offload it in the lockers outside the parks or at Marne-la-Vallee/Chessy station (situated on the first floor) during the hours after check-out and before your train leaves. This will cost much less money than Disney Express.

Scan the QR code above for the Disney Express luggage service.

The Marne-la-Vallée/Chessy station is situated right outside the entrance to the parks and the Disney Village.

BRIT TIP

Some websites may tell you that the Disney hotels will mind your bags in a secure room on the day you check out for you to return to collect later. In practice, this very rarely happens. If you are travelling on the Eurostar, the hotel porters insist that your bags are transferred to the station using the Disney Express service for you to collect from there. There is a set charge per person, usually around €5-6 less than the full cost of Disney Express. Factor this in if you know you will need to leave luggage on the final day as this could tip the balance in favour of paying that little bit more for the full service.

On the other hand, if you're on a short or weekend break during peak time when the queues are at their longest, or if you have children itching to see and do as much as possible as soon as possible, the chance to cut out the time spent getting to and checking in at the hotel could be money very well spent. If you are staying at a Partner hotel quite a distance from the parks, this is especially relevant. Also if you have older relatives or very young children in your party, consider the benefits for them of cutting out the extra walk back and forth to the hotel with luggage.

Scan the QR code to find out more about this service through the Disneyland Paris website.

Eurostar from London, to Lille, to Disneyland Paris
If the Disney Eurostar direct-link is not running on the dates of your holiday, there is another option.

Book a Eurostar from London St Pancras, Ashford or Ebbsfleet to Lille then change on to a national train service straight to Disneyland Paris. This will take between 3 and 4 hours but be sure to check prices as it may work out more expensive this way.

Eurostar from London to Gare du Nord
Another option is for you and your family to hop on to the Eurostar at London St Pancras Ashford or Ebbsfleet to arrive at Paris's international railway station, Gare du Nord, which is situated in the north of Paris in the city's tenth arrondissement or district. Change on to the RER service for Marne-la-Vallée/Chessy.

Directions from Gare du Nord to Disneyland Paris
Buy metro tickets from either the nearest manned kiosk or one of the available electronic dispensers. Each passenger will only need one ticket for the whole journey from Gare du Nord to get to the parks. Make sure you keep your tickets on you for the entire journey, as some exit barriers require you to put the ticket through again. A single ticket costs €7.60 per adult and €3.80 for children 9 and under. The journey from Gare du Nord to Disneyland Paris takes just over an hour.

■ From Gare du Nord, take the RER B train to Châtelet les Halles
■ Change at Chatelet on to the RER A train to Marne la Vallée/Chessy – this is the stop for Disneyland Paris
■ This station stands just outside of the front gates of the parks

By plane

The two main airports servicing Paris are Charles de Gaulle and Orly. One of the best and easiest ways to calculate the cheapest and most appropriate flight for your Disneyland Paris holiday is to use Google Flights – scan the QR code.

If you book through Disney, flights can be included in your overall package but while this may be nice and easy, it will not provide you with those budget deals to be found through conducting a manual search. In fact, you are much more likely to be out of pocket than if you go for the option of including Eurostar tickets in your package.

Scan the QR code above for Google Flights.

From the Airport to Disneyland Paris

By Magical Shuttle Airport Bus

This Disney-provided service takes around 45 minutes and can easily be booked even if you haven't booked your flights through Disneyland Paris. These services are available for both Charles de Gaulle and Orly guests, costing you €20 per adult and €16 per child.

By train

To get to Disneyland Paris from Charles de Gaulle Airport, first take the RER B train from Charles de Gaulle to Châtelet les Halles. Then change on to the RER A to Marne-la-Vallée/Chessy.

Orly Airport does not have a direct train to the centre of Paris, so your route will be a little more complicated. The easiest option is to book yourself on to a Magical Shuttle Airport Bus.

Otherwise, follow the directions below. This route will take you just over an hour and a half.

- ■ Leave Orly Sud, exit K, to get the CARS AF 1 Bus towards Étoile Rue Carnot
- ■ Get off at the second stop, Porte d'Orléans
- ■ Take the Metro Line 4 from Porte d'Orléans in the direction of Porte de Clignancourt, and get off at Les Halles
- ■ Change on to the RER A train at Les Halles
- ■ Hop off at Marne-la-Vallée/Chessy, and you have reached your destination!

By airport Taxi Transfers

Neither Charles de Gaulle nor Orly Airports are situated particularly near Disneyland Paris; the journey should take in the region of 45 minutes to an hour, not allowing for traffic. Roughly, you can expect a taxi from either airport to cost

BRIT TIP

Weigh up all the transfer options from your airport well in advance of your holiday to determine which best suits you – and your budget.

Scan the QR code above for transfer options to Disneyland Paris.

around €80–100 although some firms that you can pre-book in advance online may offer a better deal.

Car rental

If you are arriving by plane or train, you may want to consider hiring a car throughout your stay in Paris. This will not only give you added convenience, but will also provide a greater choice of hotel options, as not all hotels provide shuttle services to and from the parks (see chapter 3 for hotel comparisons).

Alamo is our official recommended partner for car rental. They offer cars to rent from Charles de Gaulle (Roissy) Airport and Orly Airport as well as all the major Paris train stations, with the option of dropping your car off at a different location at the end of your stay.

Scan the QR code above for the Alamo car hire website.

If you book six months in advance you can rent a car for £55 a day from Charles de Gaulle airport as opposed to £96 a day if you leave booking until a few weeks before your trip. You will also save money if you pick your car up from one of the train stations as the location charge is lower. Prices include collision damage waiver, premium location charge, vehicle license fee, VAT and unlimited mileage. Scan the QR code to visit the Alamo website for further details and to make bookings.

Hotels

Most websites and guidebooks provide information on hotels based on star ratings to give readers an idea of the quality of the hotel. However, the star rating doesn't necessarily reflect the service and hospitality of the hotel, which are essential to receiving the best hotel experience.

Choosing the best hotel

A well-appointed hotel can be ruined by the people who manage it, just as an ordinary hotel can be transformed by its great staff.

In light of this, we have carried out some exclusive research into guests' feedback on hospitality and service for a selection of hotels located within 20km of the parks. Because this feedback is so detailed and personal, we call it *ifeedback* and use it to give a hotel rating that reflects customer satisfaction. We focused on reception, room comfort, food, service and cleanliness; then we added a new measurement for its location and proximity to the parks.

We think every hotel should achieve a minimum feedback of 'good'. So, we look for better than 'good' and add bonus points where we find ratings of 'excellent' and 'very good'. Equally, we deduct points where we find feedback like 'OK' and 'poor'. It is remarkable how this hidden feedback can impact a hotel's measurement and change its standing.

We have summarised the results of our research in two tables (see pages 26 and 27) grouped in price ranges and in order of value rating. The first table shows the top choices if you are using public transport. This will either be in the form of a train station nearby or where the hotel offers a free shuttle service to the parks. The second shows the top choices if you have your own vehicle or a hire car. Most of these are still a very short drive to the parks. We have then provided a brief description of each hotel. Disney hotels are vastly more expensive compared to many of the other hotels in the listing but there are other advantages (listed on page 33) so we have included four of

TOP CHOICES BY PRICE RANGE IF USING PUBLIC TRANSPORT

	Price (average)	Ifeedback value rating
Under £100 per night		
Mariott's Village d'Ile-de-France	£75	114
Hotel Ibis Marne La Vallée Val d'Europe	£93	98
Holiday Inn Paris Marne-la-Vallée	£70	91
Campanile Marne la Vallée Bussy St Georges	£49	87
Vienna House Dream Castle Hotel	£97	84
Under £150 a night		
Hotel l'Elysée Val d'Europe	£119	104
Relais Spa Val d'Europe	£127	95
Hipark Serris Val d'Europe	£128	93
Hotel Mercure Marne-la-Vallée Bussy St Georges	£129	89
Under £175 a night		
Radisson Blu Magny Le Honge	£155	85
Vienna House Magic Circus Hotel	£150	83
From £300 upwards a night		
Disneyland Hotel	£800	97
Disney's Hotel New York	£390	88
Disney's Newport Bay Club	£380	84
Disney's Sequoia Lodge	£360	88

Scan the QR code above for our hotel comparisons web page.

the best Disney hotels as a comparison. For further details download our free scanner and use the QR code on this page to take you to up-to-date information on the Internet.

Because hotel prices go up and down throughout the year, we have taken three price points for each hotel and turned them into an average for easy comparison, so bear this in mind when you come to book your hotel.

Top choices if using public transport

Under £100 a night

Mariott's Village d'Ile-de-France
This village of one-, two- and three-bedroom townhouses is located in Bailly-Romanvilliers and looks out over the 27-

TOP CHOICES BY PRICE RANGE IF TAKING A CAR

	Price (average)	Ifeedback value rating
Under £100 per night		
Nomad Hotel Paris Roissy CDG Aeroport	£77	101
Domaine de Crécy	£95	100
Novotel Marne La Vallée Collégien	£81	96
Inter-Hôtel Meaux-Villenoy	£80	93
Paxton Resort and Spa	£93	93
Chateau de Sancy	£95	91
Under £150 a night		
Hotel Les Herbes Folles	£130	109
Hotel Oceania Paris Roissy CDG Aeroport	£114	106
Under £175 a night		
Relais du Silence Domaine de Bellevue	£150	103
Le Manoir de Gressy	£150	100

hole Golf Disneyland course. With indoor and outdoor pools, a spa, sauna, Jacuzzi and fitness centre, it's ideal for families and groups, and is a great place to unwind after a day at the Parks. Reviewers rate highly the 'simply beautiful' houses that provide separate living, sleeping and dining areas, a fully equipped kitchen and a private terrace. Each house is fitted with air conditioning, flat screen TVs, washing machine and dryer, free high-speed Wi-Fi access, hairdryer and ironing facilities.

The dining options on site are limited: Le Bistro Bar is open for breakfast, lunch and dinner and serves a variety of dishes made with locally sourced fresh produce, and the Marketplace offers snacks and groceries. Reviewers comment that these are both expensive but the local village just a short walk away provides further supermarkets and restaurants, which are better value for money.

Disneyland Paris is just four miles away and a shuttle bus runs to and from the parks for a small surcharge.

Hotel Ibis Marne La Vallée Val d'Europe
This Ibis hotel offers low prices throughout the year for basic, comfortable accommodation. Its main attraction is its location: with the Val d'Europe RER train station on

the doorstep, you can be at Disneyland Park in less than 5 minutes or in the centre of Paris in around 40 minutes. This is a good option if you come to Paris via public transport, although, if you do drive, secure underground parking is available for a fee.

All of the rooms have en-suite facilities with shower and are equipped with air conditioning, flat-screen TV and Wi-Fi but there is no kettle, fridge or safe. Despite the Ibis Hotel's central location and proximity to the trains, reviewers have commented on it being quiet.

Meals at the hotel are 'good quality and very reasonably priced' and reviewers agree at just under 10 euros the continental buffet breakfast is worth having.

Holiday Inn Paris Marne-la-Vallée

The Holiday Inn Paris Marne-la-Vallée is a modern, family-friendly hotel conveniently located near the shops and just two minutes' walk to the station. Trains from here to Disneyland Paris take about 20 minutes.

The generous-sized guest rooms can accommodate two adults and two children and are stylishly decorated. Each room has a flatscreen TV with satellite channels, tea and coffee making facilities, free high-speed WiFi and a mini bar. En-suite bathrooms have a separate bath and shower and in some cases the toilet is in a separate room. This can help save time but has been described by some reviewers as very small so you may prefer to opt for rooms where the toilet is within the bathroom.

There is a restaurant serving breakfast and dinner and a lounge bar. There is also the option to eat out at any of the nearby restaurants. One downside of staying at this hotel is the fact that the area is a bit run down and some guests have felt uncomfortable about walking back from the station late at night.

Campanile Marne-la-Vallée Bussy St Georges

This three-star hotel is a 10-minute walk to the Bussy St George station; trains run on a regular basis from here to Disneyland Paris and take 12 minutes. For most the location is very convenient, but if you have younger children, it may be worth considering whether they will be able to walk from the station after a busy day at the parks. Parking is available for car owners.

Guest rooms are equipped with air conditioning, free Wi-Fi, flat screen televisions with satellite channels and a kettle

Vienna House Dream Castle Hotel

with complimentary tea and coffee supplied. Bathrooms are modern with a shower or bath-shower combination, a hairdryer, bath towels (but no hand towels) and free toiletries. The downsides are that the rooms don't have much storage space and there are no room safes for housing valuables.

Guests can enjoy a continental breakfast at the hotel for an extra 10 euros which includes croissants, bread, cheese, cereals and fruit plus cooked sausage and eggs. The restaurant also serves a hot buffet deal, pizza or steak for the evening meal. There is a 9-acre garden and terrace area.

Vienna House Dream Castle Hotel

Just 10-minutes' to Disneyland Paris on the free shuttle bus, it's little wonder this Disney Partner hotel comes out top on our *ifeedback* for location. Themed around a European castle with French gardens and peaceful lake, the Dream Castle Hotel offers the luxury of a Disney hotel but at a fraction of the price. Guest rooms are 'spacious, quiet and comfortable' with air conditioning, free Wi-Fi, a flat screen TV, a tea and coffee welcome kit and, if requested, a mini-bar. Family rooms have curtained off bunk beds for children.

Leisure facilities include an indoor heated pool (basic and small), indoor and outdoor play areas, a spa and a fully equipped fitness centre.

The Musketeers Restaurant serves a varied buffet breakfast (worth booking in advance) and French and European cuisine for dinner. The Excalibur bar, which overlooks the hotel gardens, serves a selection of beverages and light snacks. Reviewers have commented on the 'great atmosphere' and the helpful, friendly staff who speak English.

Hotel l'Elysée Val d'Europe

Under £150 a night

Hotel l'Elysée Val d'Europe

One of the appeals of the Hotel l'Elysée Val d'Europe is that it's just a 15-minute ride on the free shuttle bus to Disneyland Paris, and a few minutes' walk from the Val d'Europe shopping centre, Sealife Aquarium and RER train station. Rooms are spacious and equipped with air conditioning, tea and coffee making facilities, flat screen TVs and complimentary WiFi; large *en-suite* bathrooms provide a bath-shower combination and hairdryer.

Guests can start the day with an American style buffet breakfast and dine in style in the evening at Le George restaurant for authentic French cuisine described by one reviewer as 'superb'. Le Diplomate café and bar offers the best of both worlds: comfortable indoor seating for a mid-morning coffee break and an outdoor heated terrace for sipping cocktails al fresco, summer and winter. The hotel has a private car park that costs E10 per day.

Relais Spa Val d'Europe

After the noise and excitement of a day at Disneyland Paris, you may just want to relax in a spa or Jacuzzi, or indulge in a massage – the Relais provides all this and more. This modern hotel is close to the popular shopping centre, Val D'Europe, and the restaurants and cafes available in this small town, as well as the metro station where you can easily catch a train into the centre of Paris. Furthermore, the Relais Spa hotel offers a free shuttle service to take you to and from Disneyland Paris in 5 to 10 minutes.

Premium rooms can sleep up to two guests and come with fully equipped kitchen, and bathroom with bath. For families

Hipark Serris Val d'Europe

up to four people you can book two connecting rooms. All rooms are elegant and cosy, and feature a flat screen TV, air conditioning and free Wi-Fi.

Breakfast, lunch and dinner are served at the onsite La Brasseries FLO restaurant, which offers a limited menu of classic regional dishes. In the evening, you can relax in the warm and cosy atmosphere of Le Franklin bar.

Hipark Serris Val d'Europe

This contemporary aparthotel offers 210 self-catering suites and studios in a good central location, close to the train station, shops, restaurants and a large supermarket (just 5 minutes' walk).

All apartments have a fully equipped kitchen – microwave, dishwasher, oven, fridge and kettle; suites also have a dining area. This makes it ideal for families who want to keep their costs down by eating in. The comfortable living area features a flat screen TV, free Wi-Fi, a work desk and a safe. Bathrooms provide a bath-shower, heated towel rail, hairdryer and complimentary toiletries. The shower has a detachable head which is useful if you don't want to get your hair wet!

The reception is open 24 hours so you don't have to worry about your arrival time; staff speak English and are helpful and friendly. There is an outdoor warm swimming pool (open from May till end of September), fitness facilities and a sauna.

The breakfast room serves continental breakfast for an additional cost.

There is secure parking under the hotel (for a fee) and a free shuttle service to the railway station and to Disneyland Paris – this runs every 15 to 45 minutes.

Hotel Mercure Marne-la-Vallée Bussy St Georges

With mixed reviews on popular travel websites, it's perhaps not surprising the Hotel Mercure has scored slightly lower on our *iFeedback*. Nevertheless, this 4-star hotel is conveniently located opposite the Bussy St George train station – just two stops and you arrive in Disneyland Paris in less than 10 minutes. All guest rooms, recently renovated, are equipped with free Wi-Fi, air conditioning, high definition TVs, fridge, safes and tea and coffee making facilities.

There is a good selection of hot and cold food for breakfast and quality French cuisine for dinner at Le Puzzle restaurant. In the evening, you can chill out to live piano music coupled with a fine wine or other chosen beverage in the lounge bar.

Under £175 a night

Radisson Blu Magny Le Honge

With a 27-hole golf course, indoor swimming pool, steam bath, sauna, gym and spa treatments this 4-star hotel offers a bit more than some of its rivals. The Pamplemousse Restaurant serves standard fare – lamb curry, fish and chips or burger and chips – and choices abound at the Super Buffet Breakfast served in the Birdie Restaurant. The Chardon Bar is open 11am to 1am for drinks and snacks; in summer months you can sit on the outdoor terrace overlooking the golf course. A 24-hour room service is also available.

Standard rooms at the Radisson are spacious and feature flat screen TVs, free Wi-Fi, a minibar, a laptop-size safe and tea and coffee making facilities.

One downside to the Radisson is that it isn't near any other shops, restaurants or takeaways so you have to eat in one of the two restaurants onsite which are fairly pricey. However, it is conveniently located for the parks and a free shuttle bus runs every 30 minutes and takes around 10 minutes. If you are going to the parks early, it's worth booking the shuttle with the concierge to guarantee a place. There is also a free car park.

Vienna House Magic Circus Hotel

Stars, stripes and warm, bold colours conjure up a circus atmosphere at this Disney partner hotel. Rooms are spacious and family-friendly with bunk beds for children and interconnecting rooms for larger families. All *en-suite* rooms have air conditioning, free high speed Internet access, a flat-screen TV with cable channels, tea and coffee supplies, room safe and mini-bar.

Vienna House Magic Circus Hotel

Other facilities include an indoor play area with games and games arcade, a heated swimming pool with a separate paddling area for little ones, a gym, and a spa for beauty treatments and massage. Guests can dine inside at L'etoile restaurant, or on the outdoor terrace (weather permitting), which looks out on the extensive grounds and lake. Alternatively, a 24-hour room service is available. Breakfast and dinner are buffet style with regional specialities, and there is a children's menu. The Bar des Artistes is open from 11am to midnight for drinks and light snacks.

The complimentary shuttle takes you to Disneyland Paris in 10 minutes and stops off at the nearby Marne-la-Vallée/Chessy train station for connections into Paris.

Disney hotels – from £300 per night

If you are looking for a once-in-a-lifetime magical experience for you and your family, the Disney hotels promise to provide that unmatchable 'Disney Difference'. Added extras such as park tickets, extra magic hours, free shuttle bus, character dining, meal plans and free parking at the hotel and parks are included in the overall cost. However, even with these incentives, prices are far and above other hotels of the same calibre and you will need to decide if you think the 'magic' is worth the expense. Our *ifeedback* research suggests the following four Disney hotels provide the best value for money.

Disneyland Hotel

You really can't get much closer to the magic than staying at the 5-star Disneyland Hotel. Reviews place this establishment among the crème de la crème of holiday choices with its elegant Victorian-inspired decor, comfortable rooms, excellent restaurant, 'superb location' and 'magical' extra features. It won the TripAdvisor Travellers' Choice Award in 2017, as one of the best French hotels for family visits. If you are looking for top of the range, with a hefty price tag to match, then Disneyland Hotel should be first on your list.

Standard rooms include free Wi-Fi, air conditioning, in-room safe, hair dryer, bathrobe and slippers. Castle club rooms and suites have the added benefits of a private reception desk and access to a private lounge open from 7.30am to 11pm serving hot and cold drinks. The classic and luxury family rooms can sleep up to five people.

Disneyland Hotel boasts a heated indoor pool suitable for all the family and a full-service gym. Guests can also relax and unwind in the Jacuzzi or steam bath, or indulge in various massage and beauty treatments (for an additional cost) at the Celestia Spa.

There are two restaurants to choose from at Disneyland Hotel. At Inventions, you can enjoy a buffet of international cuisine for around €65 per adult, €35 per child, and get to meet some of the Disney characters who talk to guests, sign autographs and pose for one or two photographs. Alternatively, take a seat overlooking Main Street USA and sample the West Coast-inspired menu of the California Grill restaurant. With a semi-formal dress code, a wine cellar boasting bottles to suit any chosen menu, and star chef Philippe Geneletti on hand to turn your order into a reality, this eatery really tries to bring a taste of adult dining into the youthful Disney setting. However, with just the main course costing from €50 to €66 per person, reviews comment on the high price, and the possibility of getting more for your money at Inventions just down the corridor.

Café Fantasia, a calming piano bar, allows you to sit back and unwind after the hustle and bustle of a day in the Parks.

Disney's Hotel New York

At a short distance from the Parks, either by walking or by the free shuttle bus service, the Hotel New York is ideally located for a family trip to Disneyland Paris. The focus moves across the pond to the Big Apple, with its lights, skyscrapers and Art Deco styling. A few previous guests have noted the need for 'a refresh' on the interiors that can seem 'a bit dated', and its high rates put it lower down on our *ifeedback* for value for money. Nevertheless, rooms provide all the mod cons – flat screen TV, coffee maker and free Wi-Fi. The hotel boasts an indoor – outdoor swimming pool, a fitness centre, tennis court, steam room and sauna.

For that Central Park feel, dine onsite at the Manhattan Restaurant where you will be served a cosmopolitan meal complete with jazz soundtrack and soft lighting. Reviews praise the 'fine food' and 'first class service' to be found at this up-market eatery, even if you do sacrifice a little on the Disney setting and magical backdrop.

Alternatively, step inside The Parkside Diner for a varied buffet including salads, seafood, charcuterie and child-friendly options. The elegant New York-themed cocktail bar offers a place to relax and unwind after a busy day at the Parks.

Disney's Sequoia Lodge

Just across the waters of Lake Disney from the Disney Village, Sequoia Lodge is conveniently placed with a free shuttle service to take you to the parks. This establishment offers its guests the feel of a warm and cosy mountainside lodge amidst a woodland setting, with one reviewer describing the 'the whole experience [as] just perfect and magical'.

All rooms sleep up to four people and are themed around Bambi and friends. Standard rooms include radio and TV, hair dryer, free Wi-Fi and kettle (on request) but buffet breakfast is not included. Club rooms and suites have a few extra perks such as a mini-fridge, access to the private lounge and American buffet breakfast.

Step inside **The Hunter's Grill and Beaver Creek Taver**n to sample a selection of meats and homely foods on offer in this all-you-can-eat buffet. This eatery may not boast the same elegant settings as the restaurants in either Hotel New York or the Newport Bay Club, but what it lacks in luxury it makes up for in value for money. Adults pay between €30 and €35 per person, whilst the kid's plates (for 3 to 11s) set you back between €15 and €20 each. This eatery can get busy in high season, so try to book ahead through the Dining Reservation Service on +33 1 60 30 40 50.

Guests have plenty of opportunities to relax and unwind: take a dip in the pool, indulge in a sauna or work out at the gym. When evening comes, head to the **Redwood Bar and Lounge** for drinks and bar snacks.

Disney's Newport Bay Club

Disney's Newport Bay Club embraces the feel of an elite maritime waterfront mansion. Renovated in spring 2016, this luxurious 1920s-inspired building has a slight upper hand on its New York-themed neighbour if only for its fresh and updated appearance. You can either enjoy the 15-minute walk to the Parks or take the free shuttle bus straight to the gates.

All rooms have a nautical theme: standard rooms sleep up to four people; family rooms up to five people and compass club family rooms up to six people. Amenities include free WiFi, TV, hair dryer, air conditioning, luggage service and kettle (upon request). American buffet breakfast is included in Club Rooms as well as access to the private lounge.

Boasting a selection of international and Mediterranean dishes, Newport Bay Club's **Cape Cod** restaurant prides itself on the quality and variety of its seafood. At between €30 and €35 per adult, and €15 to €20 per child, the buffet offers many salad and dessert options, with reviewers commenting on the 'exotic' selection to try. Other guests have been slightly put off by the queues found at the door of this restaurant however, so make sure you book ahead through the Dining Reservation Service on +33 1 60 30 40 50.

Mediterranean dishes meet New England in **The Yacht Club** table-service restaurant. Costing between €30 and €40 per person for a set menu, this oceanic eatery again takes seafood as its main offering, but also offers an impressively broad menu including vegetarian dishes and a buffet-style children's menu. Varied reviews from previous guests comment on the luxurious 'feel of New England' and the 'excellent food and service', even if the prices are (like so many Disney Hotel restaurants) a little on the steep side.

Finish your day with a drink at the Newport Bay Club's bar, **Captain's Quarters**. Sit back with a whisky, cocktail or another beverage of your choice to steady yourself after your theme park adventure.

Other amenities include heated indoor and outdoor pools, a sauna and steam bath and full-service gym.

Top choices if you have a car

Under £100 a night

Nomad Hotel Paris Roissy CDG Aeroport

The Nomad is a modern, uncluttered and functional hotel about 28 miles from Disneyland Paris. It is best to have your own transport, as trains from the airport to Marne-la-Vallée are infrequent. Parking is available on site for €15 a day.

Nomad guest rooms are small but comfortable and feature movable and multi-function bedding to suit your needs. You can also adjust the lighting, heating, air conditioning, video projector and roller blinds all with the touch screen tablet provided. Even the see-through shower cubicle offers three settings, including massage jets, as well as mood lighting.

The décor throughout the Nomad Hotel is Scandinavian in style using natural materials and accents of colour. A varied buffet breakfast is served from 6am to 11am; reasonably priced dinner from 7pm to 10pm and a large selection of beverages at the bar any time of the day or night.

With many reviewers commenting on the 'kind and helpful staff', it's not surprising this has scored highly on our *iFeedback*.

Domaine de Crécy

If you're looking for somewhere quiet and rural but close enough to the parks, then Domaine de Crécy is ideally situated. This tastefully restored 17th century stone farmhouse, located in the heart of Brie, provides 29 spacious and comfortable apartments for up to six guests. These feature a living area with TV with satellite channels, bathroom with shower/bath combination and a kitchenette with refrigerator, microwave and electric hob. Bedrooms have blackout curtains. There is also free WiFi, although reviewers say the signal is poor.

Domaine de Crécy

Outside amenities include a seasonal swimming pool, two golf courses and a tennis court; there is free parking on-site.

Le Panoramic restaurant serves a continental buffet breakfast (ordered on request), lunch and dinner. All produce is fresh and locally sourced and a children's menu is available. If you prefer to cater for yourself, there is a supermarket in the nearby village, Crécy-la-Chapelle.

Disneyland Paris is about a 20-minute drive away.

Novotel Marne La Vallée Collégien

Guest rooms at the Novotel are modern, clean and spacious and can sleep up to four people. They are equipped with queen size beds, free Wi-Fi, LED TV, kettle and safe. En-suite facilities include a bath or shower and a separate toilet.

The Novotel is family-friendly offering free accommodation and breakfast for two children under 16, safe play areas and a children's menu. There is also an indoor playground, an outdoor, unheated pool and a video games area.

The Novotel Café serves a varied buffet breakfast and French cuisine for lunch and dinner. Guests can also relax at the bar or grab a quick snack at the 24-hour self-service snack bar.

Given its convenient location for Disneyland Paris (less than 15-minutes' drive away) and friendly and helpful staff, the Novotel offers good value for money.

Inter-Hôtel Meaux-Villenoy

This hotel is on an industrial estate on the former site of the sugar factory. Despite the surroundings not being that aesthetic, reviewers have commented on it being in a 'safe' location and very convenient for getting to Disneyland Paris – just a 20-minute drive. The hotel has a large car park which is free to guests. The downside for those without transport is that there isn't much entertainment at the hotel and it takes 10 to 15 minutes to walk to the town and station.

Although basic, rooms are clean, tasteful and larger than the usual French economy hotels. The domestic rooms for four people are particularly good value for money. All rooms are non-smoking and feature free Wi-Fi, an LED TV and desk but no kettle or fridge. The private bathrooms have efficient rain showers (no baths) and a hairdryer. Guests can enjoy a continental breakfast in the modern breakfast room which is light and airy. Rooms are available from 3pm on the day of your arrival; reception staff are 'friendly and accommodating'.

Paxton Resort and Spa

Paxton Resort and Spa is modern and elegant in style and features 232 contemporary and spacious rooms. Standard double and twin rooms feature LCD TV with satellite channels, free Wi-Fi, air conditioning and in-room safe. There is also a small kitchenette with fridge and microwave, and kitchenware is available to hire for an extra cost.

A continental breakfast, included in the price, is served between 6.30 and 10.30am each morning. The choice is plentiful – croissants, cereal, toast, beans, boiled eggs and frankfurters. For dinner, guests can enjoy a genuine Italian at L'Origano served in the plush restaurant or on the outside terrace. Dishes include homemade pasta, risottos and wood-fired pizzas.

The energetic members of the family can compete at 10-pin bowling in the 20-lane alley adjacent to The Crystal Bar or take part in a game of billiards. If you prefer something more relaxing, unwind in the cosy atmosphere of The Spirit lounge bar, take a dip in the indoor pool or indulge in any massage or beauty treatment at the spa.

The Paxton Resort and Spa is only 10 minutes away from Disneyland Paris by car. There is a free shuttle bus but it only takes you to the local train station where you can then catch a train to Disneyland Paris. For this reason, we think it would suit those with their own form of transport better.

Reviewers have commented on the 'friendly and helpful staff' and the 'excellent value for money'.

Chateau de Sancy

Set in eight acres of grounds, the Chateau de Sancy offers the peace and quiet of the countryside but is just a short drive (20 minutes) to the parks. Facilities include table tennis equipment, an outdoor tennis court, heated indoor pool, mountain bikes and an equestrian centre. There is also a nearby golf course – if you would like a game, contact the hotel to reserve a place before your arrival.

All 21 rooms are spacious, soundproofed and charmingly furnished. Each room is fitted with a flat screen TV, free Wi-Fi, minibar and in-room safe. The *en suite* bathrooms are modern and offer a bath-shower combination, hair dryer and complimentary toiletries, bathrobes and slippers. Suites with pull-out sofa beds are available for larger groups.

For an extra charge, guests can enjoy a continental buffet breakfast at La Table Du Chateau. Dinner is served here, or on the outside terrace, and features French cuisine made from locally sourced ingredients. The lounge bar offers a relaxing evening atmosphere with live piano music. The Chateau offers two free on-site parking areas.

Under £150 a night

Hotel Les Herbes Folles

Located in Mauregard, a small village 10-minutes' drive from the Charles de Gaule airport, Les Herbes Folles offers modern comfort in rural surroundings. The 'welcoming and accommodating' staff and 'great customer service' consistently impress reviewers earning it a high place in our *iFeedback*. Couples in particular like this location.

Stylish and elegant rooms feature vibrant, designer fabrics and offer WiFi with good Internet connection, flatscreen TV and a choice of bath or shower. Soundproofing in each room means you won't be disturbed by plane noise but summer months can be uncomfortably hot as there is no air conditioning.

The bistro restaurant offers 'excellent dinners from a simple menu and adequate self-serve breakfast' in traditional French style. There is also a separate bar/lounge. In fine weather, guests can relax on the terrace and admire the beautiful garden, or go for a free bike ride using the onsite bicycles provided.

There is free onsite parking and a shuttle service to the airport; Disneyland Paris is a 30-minute drive away.

Hotel Oceania Paris Roissy CDG Aeroport
The Hotel Oceania is right next door to the Nomad and provides similar accommodation. Parking is available on site and costs €14 a day.

Taking pride of place is Oceania's fabulous swimming pool; take a dip, work out in the gym or enjoy the massage, steam rooms or Jacuzzi.

Rooms are quiet and comfortable with state-of-the-art features including climate control, flat screen TVs, powerful showers and free WiFi; some also have coffee machines. One reviewer has described the Nautilus Restaurant adjoining the hotel as 'outstanding' and the food 'superb'. Lunch, dinner and a varied buffet breakfast are all available here and drinks are served at the lounge bar in the evenings. With 'friendly and welcoming' staff, the Oceania is a good option if you don't mind being a bit further away from the parks than other hotels are.

Under £175 a night
Relais du Silence Domaine de Bellevue
This beautifully renovated farmhouse set in the countryside, with views over fields and a landscaped garden, is the perfect antidote to a day out in Disneyland Paris.

With tasteful and unique décor, all guest rooms feature a living area, flat screen TV, air conditioning, hairdryer and en-suite bath or shower. Deluxe suites include a four-poster bed, Wi-Fi and mini bar, and some have a private terrace with outside seating; others access to the spa.

The 'very helpful and obliging staff' at the Relais du Silence will go out of their way to provide an excellent service, and speak fluent English. Guests can enjoy fresh, seasonal produce at the brasserie restaurant – described by one reviewer as 'gorgeous' – and buffet breakfast on the veranda.

To relax completely, head to the spa for massage treatment, steam room, sauna and Jacuzzi or take a stroll down the quiet country lanes.

The Relais du Silence is located in Neufmoutiers-en-Brie just 12km from Disneyland Paris – about a 25-minute drive – and 45km from the capital. There is free parking on site.

Le Manoir de Gressy

This manor-house hotel has 85 luxury rooms with balconies, and 31 with a private terrace; French doors lead out to the Italian gardens and heated pool. Guest rooms, classically decorated with shabby chic furniture and fabric are spacious and comfortable. Each room is fitted with satellite television and complimentary Wi-Fi and bathrooms are modern in style with a shower or a shower-bath combination and heated towel rails.

Guests can start the day with an 'outstanding' buffet breakfast served in Le Cellier du Manoir. Fine French cuisine is served buffet-style for lunch and dinner and has been described by one reviewer as 'lavish' with 'so many choices and all delectable'.

Other facilities include a spa offering beauty treatments and massage, a gym, three tennis courts and a sauna.

Pets are welcome at this hotel and there is free parking for guests. It's advisable to have your own car as the Le Manoir de Gressy is remote from other services; nevertheless it's just a 10-minute drive from Roissy Charles de Gaulle Airport and 20 minutes' drive to Disneyland Paris.

Tips on booking a hotel

- Hotel search websites show their prices per room and not per person, so make sure you calculate this accordingly.

- The more nights you stay, the cheaper each night is – it's simple really! Take this into account when looking at our 'Top Choices' tables on pages 26–27, as these prices are all for single night stays, and therefore show the room at its most expensive rate per night.

■ The date you arrive will determine the price for the rest of your stay. This will work in your favour if you have one night in a lower priced season and the rest in a higher but will not be to your advantage the other way around. In this instance you can change your dates or book one package for the expensive night and another for the cheaper nights.

■ Each hotel offers something a little different. We have provided a summary of each hotel's amenities and features but you can use the QR code we provide on page 25 for further information and to check out the deal for yourself before booking.

■ Prices for hotels online fluctuate constantly – which can be great for finding a one-off deal for your trip! This does mean, however, that, some of the best deals are only around for a day or so at a time.

■ Check what age a child is defined as for any given hotel. Most hotels define a child as being between 3 and 11 years of age, meaning that children under 3 are usually free, and those classed as children get a reduced rate. However, some hotels allow children under 7 in for free, so keep your eyes open to save yourself some money.

■ Booking over the phone is an alternative to online booking. It has the advantage of allowing you to pay in instalments rather than in one lump sum and of being able to modify your booking (such as adding extra meal vouchers) up until you have paid the final amount.

■ In France there is a city tax added to the price of your hotel room, and it is usually calculated per person, per night. Hotel search websites won't usually add this small amount – or any added VAT – until the checkout stage, so keep your eye on the price and double check the small print.

■ Finally, all hotel search sites like to include booking fees. This is normally just a couple of euros added on to the price of your hotel before you reach the checkout. The worst culprit for this is Disneyland Paris themselves: they serve their customers with a whopping €19 charge per reservation!

Buying tickets

If you are not booking your holiday through Disney or taking up one of the independent package options, the next stage in the building of your Disneyland Paris holiday is booking your tickets.

Pre-booking tickets to the parks themselves is essential – arriving expecting to pay the day rate on the gate is likely to turn out to be by far the most expensive option, and will certainly mean you start your day in a very long queue.

Ticket types
See the tables on pages 44 and 45 for a helpful breakdown of the types of ticket available for you and your family depending on the number of days and the ages of those in your group.

Making the best choice for your needs
These tips are best used if you are planning on staying in a non-Disney hotel, and therefore do not have the tickets bundled into a helpful, but pricey, package:

- Buying two Mini day tickets in a row is not the same as buying a two-day pass. Actually, because Mini day tickets are weekday restricted access it is much cheaper to buy two Mini day tickets back to back than buying a multi-day pass for 2 days. You will be saving around €15 per person.
- Rather than buying a 3-day or a 4-day pass for your Disneyland Paris visit, you might as well buy an Annual Pass for you and the members of your family. As the table above shows, a child's 3-day ticket is going to cost you a minimum of €158, whilst an Annual Classic ticket is only €135: buying an annual pass has already saved you €23! And then you might decide to come back again later in the year, making this little trick even more of a money-saver.
- Look out for the various deals going on throughout the year, especially during the off-peak season (January to March) when the best 2-for-1 park tickets are usually available.

TYPE OF TICKET		INCLUDES	
Mini		1 day weekday visits, excluding restricted dates	
Magic		1 day visit, any day	
Super Magic		1 day anytime visits, *including weekends* and excluding restricted dates	
Super Magic +		1 day visit, any day (restrictions apply)	
2 day		Unlimited access for 2 consecutive days	
3 day		Unlimited access for 3 consecutive days	
4 day		Unlimited access for 4 consecutive days	
Annual (buy onsite or over the phone at 0800 44800898)	Discovery	150 days of admission, with car parking available for €40	
	Magic Flex	300 days of admission, with car parking and shop discounts	
	Magic Plus	350 days of admission, with car parking, shop and restaurant discounts and other perks	
	Infinity	365 days of admission, with privileged car parking, shop, and restaurant discounts and a range of extra perks	

NB: All prices subject to fluctuation. For more detailed information about what each of these ticket options include, scan the QR code to visit the Disneyland Paris ticket page on their website.

■ If you are prepared to use the French Disneyland Paris website to book your holiday you could save a lot of money. At least have a look at it to see if this works for you.

PRICE FOR 1 PARK		PRICE FOR BOTH PARKS	
Age 3-11	Age 12+	Age 3-11	Age 12+
€36/£32	€43/£38	€53/£48	€60/£53
€48/£43	€55/£49	€67/£59	€72/£64
€57/£51	€63/£56	€74/£66	€81/£72
€62/£55	€69/£61	€79/£70	€85/£76
NA – these tickets always include both parks		€115/£102	€130/£116
		€144/£128	€159/£142
		€156/£139	€196/£174
€139 per person			
€189 per person			
€249 per person			
€399 per person			

Entrance to Disneyland Paris.

Best ticket deals

If you are planning to scour the internet for the best ticket deals for the parks, proceed with caution! There aren't many different outlets online that legitimately sell tickets

Based on the price for 1 person staying for 1 night in a room for 2 adults, and having Disneyland Paris tickets for 2 days	Disneyland Paris website: hotel and tickets	
Dream Castle Hotel	€270	
Radisson Blu Hotel	€332	
Algonquin's Explorers Hotel	€283	
B&B Hotel	€215	

Scan the QR code above for the Attractiontix website.

Scan the QR code above for the Attraction Tickets Direct website.

for cheaper than Disneyland Paris. The following two sites, however, may be able to provide you with the best, most trustworthy, deals outside of the Disneyland Paris website, and booking through either of them will help you to avoid falling foul of a scam: attractiontix.co.uk and attraction-tickets-direct.co.uk (scan the QR codes for their websites).

Best combined hotel and park tickets

When it comes to piecing together your Disneyland Paris holiday, you need to take into account the prices of both your hotel and the park tickets combined.

The easiest and quickest way to create a package deal is to go through the Disneyland Paris website – but be warned, this is in no way the cheapest way to buy the holiday for you and your family.

Disney Hotels

You cannot stay in the Disney Hotels without having the tickets included in the overall package. Prices vary throughout the year but include:

- Your room
- Disney park tickets (if you stay 1 night you get tickets for 2 days)
- Access to all attractions and shows throughout the parks
- Access to Meet & Greets / meals with Disney characters
- A free Shuttle bus to and from your hotel
- Free parking at your hotel and at the parks

Please note that as of 2017, breakfast is no longer included in the Disney hotel package and is charged extra. Keep your eye on the Disneyland Paris website for special deals on these packages throughout the year, and equally use Lastminute. com for some of the best spot deals available. Common deals include 30 to 35% off the price of park tickets or receiving extra free nights added on to your overall stay.

Price for hotel only on Expedia for the same dates	Price of two mini day tickets (see ticket tips above)	Total price for hotel and tickets	YOU SAVE
€80.50	€124	€204.50	**€70.50**
€79.50		€203.50	**€128.50**
€53.50		€177.50	**€105.50**
€59		€183	**€32**

Partner Hotels

There are two main ways to book rooms at the Partner Hotels: the first is through the Disneyland Paris website, and the other way is either directly through the hotel website or through a hotel search website.

The chart above shows how the prices of these two compare.

Booking your hotel and park tickets separately and using our money-saving Ticket Tips really does cut back on the overall expense.

Other Hotels

Making a DIY package by combining the prices that you want is the best way to save you money, and this applies to all of the non-Disney hotels. There is a simple step-by-step way to create the best value Disneyland Paris package, and it is:

- Use our 'Top Choices by price range' tables and hotel descriptions in chapter three to select the hotel that best fulfils the requirements of your family and your budget.
- Use the hotel search websites to search for the best deals.
- Depending on how many days you want to visit the parks, book either single or multi-day tickets – or annual passes to save yourself even more money.
- Follow our money saving tips to cut down your spending when you are there.

5 At the parks

If this is your first visit to Disneyland Paris, or perhaps if you are on a short break, or sharing the break with relatives or friends, one of the best things you can do before you head for the parks is take some time to think through your priorities and get a plan in mind.

Consider the particular requirements, likes and dislikes of your own family. Do you have young children who want to meet as many characters as possible? Perhaps you have a toddler and a much older child whose 'wish lists' for the holiday are very different. Do you have older relatives with you who might want to take a break for a sit-down meal at lunchtime? By considering all the options in advance and prioritising what is most important to you, you can make sure you start on the right track and stick to it right through your holiday.

Equally, it is advisable to have a budget and to look at the optional extras in advance so that you can decide in the cold light of day if they are worth the money and right for you. Being confronted with an unplanned extra and having to decide then and there whether or not to go for it is the easiest way to fall into the trap of spending more than you intended.

Here are a few pointers on ways to save both time and money at the parks, plus some information on where to meet the characters, what dining options are available and how to choose the most suitable rides for your family.

Saving time

Itineraries

To help you plan, we've devised a number of itineraries to cater for different family groups. Simply scan in the QR code here to access them. All itineraries are based upon a 3-night stay during August without Extra Magic Hours, with access to both parks. Many families will choose to split up and follow

Scan the QR code above for our itineries.

Sleeping Beauty castle

different itineraries to suit different aged children. With this in mind, most of the itineraries have certain timed events in common, including mealtimes, the parade and Disney Illuminations. Check these before you set off and agree your meeting points in the specified locations.

The FastPass system

Scan the QR code above for the Disneyland Paris' FastPass web page.

We can all agree that standing in what sometimes feel like endless queues for rides at theme parks is frustrating, boring (especially for children) and the biggest waste of valuable holiday time. Unfortunately, especially during the summer peak season or around Christmas-time, to some extent this is the nature of the beast and it would be unrealistic to try to suggest that there is any way that you can avoid queues entirely. If you have decided to go to Disneyland Paris during the school summer holidays, you will need to go already prepared to have to queue – and to have packed some patience along with your passport! Some of the rides and attractions are infamous for their long queues, most notably **Star Wars Hyperspace Mountain**, **Crush's Coaster**, **Big Thunder Mountain**, **Ratatouille: The Adventure**, **RC Racer**, **Peter Pan's Flight** and **Dumbo the Flying Elephant**, but queues of surprising length can build up just about anywhere.

One way to beat some of the crowds is to make full use of the FastPass system. The first thing to understand about FastPass is that, despite the similarity in name, it is not the same as the 'virtual queue' systems in use in UK theme parks like Alton Towers and Chessington World Of Adventures for which you have to pay an additional, often exorbitantly expensive, extra fee per person. FastPass at Disneyland Paris is FREE – and it is surprising how many visitors from the UK simply don't realise this at first.

Not all the rides offer FastPasses, but where they do, here's how they work:

- At the entrance to the ride, look up at the digital FastPass time boards. They will tell you the time that they are currently issuing FastPasses for. Do not be surprised if this is hours away. Decide if the time available will suit you and if so go up to the booth to get your FastPasses.
- Insert your park ticket into one of the FastPass machines. You will need the park ticket for each member of your family who wants a FastPass.
- The machine will then return your park ticket to you and issue a FastPass ticket with the time you need to return on it for your allotted ride.

■ Come back at this time to get on the ride within minutes, beating those time-consuming queues!

Note that the ticket will only be accepted within the 30-minute window stated on the ticket so make sure it does not clash with a show, parade or dining reservation you already have for the same time. Once you are holding a FastPass you cannot obtain another one until either you have used it – or two hours have passed since it was issued. You can, however, hold FastPass tickets for a Disneyland Park and Walt Disney Studios park attraction at the same time. Tickets often run out before the end of the day, and on the most popular rides may even be gone by mid-morning so it's important to get them at the first opportunity if you really want to experience that ride.

Single Rider

Some of the popular rides, including **Ratatouille: The Adventure** and **Crush's Coaster**, offer a **Single Rider Service** which can help cut down the time spent queuing if you aren't worried about being split up from your friends or family on the ride. As the name suggests, single riders are placed in the next available single seat.

The Single Rider queue invariably does move faster than the regular one but make sure you check the wait time indicator at the entrance to the attraction to assess whether it will save you time or not. There is not usually a shortage of people willing to hop on a ride by themselves and this means that at peak times the Single Rider queue can be as little as 5 minutes shorter than the regular queue.

Baby Switch

If you and your partner have a baby or young child but you both still want to have a go on the rides, there is an excellent **Baby Switch** queuing system in place at Disneyland Paris. On many rides including, but not limited to, **Star Wars Hyperspace Mountain**, **Big Thunder Mountain** and **The Twilight Zone Tower of Terror**, one parent can get on the ride whilst the other stays with the child. The parents then switch places without having to queue a second time. Inform the Cast Member at the entrance to the ride that you want to use Baby Switch and they will let you know the procedure. Be aware that the arrangement procedures differ from ride to ride (sometimes they issue tickets; sometimes they allow the second parent to enter through the disabled access and so on) so always check before you join the queue to make sure you have followed the procedure correctly.

Scan the QR code above for the Disneyland Paris' Baby Switch web page.

BRIT TIP

If you approach a ride during the **Extra Magic Hours** and the queue looks longer than you might have hoped, move on to something else – and then try coming back just before or after official opening time. Sometimes everyone has the same idea and rushes for the slow-loaders, making the queue as long as ever. Often this crowd will have died down towards the end of the Extra Magic Hours – and you'll be ahead of everyone just entering the park.

Disney Extra Magic Hours

A big perk of staying at a Disney hotel is the Extra Magic Hours bonus. If you show your hotel room key or hotel ID card you can get entry to certain areas of the parks up to two hours before official opening time. At busy times of year this is a great way to jump on a ride well ahead of the crowds – if whizzing round on a rollercoaster at 8am is your thing, of course!

Shop early – or late

Beat the crowds by completing all your gift and merchandise shopping early in the day, whether in the parks or at Disney Village. You can enter either of the parks' shopping areas thirty minutes earlier than the official opening times – an ideal time to shop. You can then request the hands-free shopping service that allows you to pick up your purchases, without having to carry them around the park. If you are staying in a Disney hotel the shop will transfer your shopping to your hotel for you to pick up, usually from the hotel shop.

Alternatively, wait until the end of the day to shop. Shops on Main Street stay open for about an hour after the official park closing time and Disney Village shops are open until midnight on most days.

Plan your meal times

If you casually wander off to a restaurant at 12.30pm or 6pm because rumbling stomachs tell you it's time, you can be sure you will join the rest of the crowds with the same idea. At peak times it can be impossible to get a table in a sit-down restaurant and no one likes queuing just to get into one. Counter service options are just as bad, with wait times of 45 minutes or longer. With a little forward-thinking, you can find plenty of ways to ensure that this problem never troubles you. Here are some tips:

- The lunchtime rush in both parks lasts from midday to 2.30pm. Have a light breakfast so you can head to lunch early (anytime from 11am) or alternatively fill up at breakfast so that you are not ready for lunch until after 2.30pm.
- If you want to dine at a table service restaurant for lunch, book it at least at the beginning of the day, or as far in advance as you can if you are a table larger than 4.
- If you are on a breakfast package, consider having a large breakfast and making use of quick snacks like ice cream, popcorn or fruit to keep you going until mid-afternoon. If you can eat a proper meal at around 4pm you will bypass the traditional 'lunch and dinner' routine skipping both the

crowds and the need to take time out for two meals. Plus, you should be out of the restaurant just in time for the daily parade, if that's on your list!

- Head out of the parks (don't forget to get your hand stamped so you can return later) and eat at any of the restaurants or cafes at Disney Village. They are quieter than the parks at lunchtime, extremely quiet in mid-afternoon – but beware! – they will be very busy at dinnertime.
- Avoid any of the eateries either in Main Street USA or along the path of the parade just before and just after the event.
- If you aren't interested in the parade or are planning to see it on another day, then you can usually save time by going to one of the eateries while it is happening. Queues are much shorter and the restaurants are always less crowded during this period as many of the other guests are out watching the characters march by, or making use of the shorter ride queues.
- If you have your own packed lunch with you, the only thing you will have to wait for is an available bench!
- Most of the restaurants in the Disney Hotels open late for guests, but if you are looking to eat at one of the restaurants in the park for your dinnertime meal, make sure you plan ahead. If the park is closing at around 10pm, book your table through the Dining Reservation Service on +33 1 60 30 40 50 for around 7.30pm to make sure you can get through the meal and back to the Central Plaza in time for the Disney Illuminations fireworks display.

Saving money

Bring your own food

Despite what some guidebooks might say, you are allowed to bring your own food and drink into the parks. You aren't allowed to sit on the lawns to eat it but there are plenty of benches scattered about. A rucksack filled with such items as sandwiches, fruit, snacks, water and other drinks is fine as long as you don't have alcoholic beverages or anything in glass containers (apart from baby food). Group picnics that require specific equipment such as cool boxes, tables and containers are only allowed to take place in the designated picnic area to the side of the entrance walkway from the main parking lot.

The Auchan hypermarket in Val d'Europe is an excellent option for good quality, inexpensive picnic food. If you go to the rear of the supermarket on the ground floor beyond the bakery you will find all their discounted food items in one place. Here you can get bags of 12 pain au chocolat or croissants for the same price as four in a bag from the bakery, cereals, fresh cheese, bread, juice and yoghurts are all cheaper than those in the main aisles. Fruit is in a different section and needs to be weighed and priced before taking to the checkout.

There is also a mini-market at the Marne-la-Vallee/Chessy train station selling all the essentials. Bringing your own food to the parks will be a particularly significant saving for larger families, and it will keep you healthy and hydrated throughout the day – you can even fill your water bottle at any of the many drinking fountains provided in both parks.

Half-board meal plans

If you want to eat at the various table- or buffet-service restaurants throughout the parks and the Disney Village during your stay, the half-board meal plan can save you up to 15% off the price of those meals. Do your research on this well in advance and unless it is included in your package as a free perk, make sure it's right for you before you book it. If you are interested, note that you will need to book this along with your hotel and park tickets, you can't add it on later.

Skip lunch

Avoiding the traditional breakfast, lunch and dinner routine, as well as saving a lot of time (see pages 52–53) will also save you a lot of money. If breakfast is included in your hotel package make this a proper meal that will keep you going into the afternoon. Disney hotels now charge extra for breakfast when you book so make the most of it. All the Disney hotels offer an excellent continental breakfast spread including cheese and charcuterie, and most have a hot buffet too offering items such as scrambled eggs, sausages and sauté potatoes. It stands to reason that if you make the most of what's on offer at breakfast and perhaps with an ice-cream or small snack along the way you can then skip lunch and go for an early dinner at around 4pm, you will be cutting out the price of a whole meal per day. In the parks, this is a significant saving.

Take your own photos

Taking your own photos is the cheapest option although it's unlikely you will be able to take any on the faster thrill rides. Disney offer on-ride photos on **Big Thunder Mountain, Star Wars Hyperspace Mountain, The Twilight Zone Tower of Terror, Pirates of the Caribbean, Buzz Lightyear Laser Blast** and **Rock 'n Roller Coaster** to capture riders' reactions at the crucial moment. They can be purchased as souvenirs in a variety of formats from framed prints to key rings, mugs and calendars from €15 upwards. Go to the video screens as you exit the ride to find your photo, make a note of its number and head to the collection desk near to the exit if you want to make a purchase.

There are always professional photographers at character meet and greets but the accompanying Cast Member will be happy to capture the moment for you with your own camera, or you are welcome to stand alongside and snap as many photos as you like. The characters, especially the costumed ones like Mickey Mouse or Woody, will pose and play along for you if you engage with them so there is often no need to spend extra on these official shots.

PhotoPass+

If you do decide to buy a number of character and ride photos, it may work out cheaper for you to pay for the PhotoPass+ package for your entire family for €49.99, rather than buy them individually. The package includes having all of these pictures sent to you online for you to check out at home and to create a photo album from them. Scan the QR code for more details.

Scan the QR code above for more information about PhotoPass.

Take kids fancy dress with you

Many young children dress up as their favourite Disney character for their visit to Disneyland Paris. Not just for Disney character meals, but also for the meet-and-greets and just around the parks generally, kids feel extra-special and get extra attention from the characters when they are in costume. Bear in mind that the cost of Disney fancy dress is Paris is far higher than we are used to spending in the UK. Children's outfits, often including accessories, can cost from as little as £14 from UK retailers, while in the parks you can expect something like a Disney princess dress to cost in the region of €70 – without accessories! It's certainly true that the Disneyland version will be far superior in design, detail and quality of fabric but if this won't bother your child, consider whether you'd prefer to make space in the suitcase to bring an outfit from home.

Meet the Characters

For many, of course young children but actually plenty of grown-ups too!, meeting the characters is a highlight of their trip to Disneyland Paris. If this is going to be a big thing for your family, plan the character meet-and-greets into your

day and visit the specific locations in Disneyland Park and Walt Disney Studios where they can be found.

Queues can be long, of course, but if your little prince or princess wants to enjoy their special moment with a character the formal meet-and-greets do offer many advantages. For a start, once you have joined a queue you are guaranteed to meet that character; a Cast Member may close the queue behind you to prevent others from joining, but if you are in it, you will never be turned away. The formal meet-and-greet settings also offer a quiet and civilised few minutes just for you. Whatever you want within reason (maybe a hug, a high-five or an autograph) will be accommodated and you will not feel rushed at all. Finally, although there are open character appearances in certain areas of the parks at set times which are published in the daily entertainment guide – and if you're very lucky these can be great little moments – in general you can expect an awful lot of jostling and pushing to get to the characters once they appear amongst you. There will always be people who will forget their manners in those situations, and that can be stressful and upsetting, especially for children. If it is important to your children to meet the characters it is best not to rely solely on these encounters but to set time aside in your day for an individual meet-and-greet.

If your child is meeting their particular favourite character, take some of your merchandise of that character with you, for example your child's cuddly toy Winnie the Pooh to meet Winne himself. You could dress up as the Princess you are meeting, or perhaps even just wear a themed T-shirt for your meet-and-greet. The characters seize upon any details that are appropriate to their character and really use them to interact with children and will spend time playing with their cuddly toys or trying on hats or accessories. This can make this a magical personal experience, especially for very young children.

A bonus for Disney hotel guests is the reintroduction in 2017 of character meet-and-greets each morning in the Disney hotels. Previously a Disney hotel staple, many regular visitors were dismayed when this practice was discontinued in 2015. Happily, it was back by popular demand for the 25th Anniversary celebrations so if you are staying in a Disney hotel you can expect to meet Mickey, Minnie, Goofy and Pluto each morning in your hotel lobby.

Your daily entertainment guide on the reverse of your park map will provide details of the character meet-and-greet times and locations for the day, and be aware that these do vary throughout the year. For a handy guide though, up-to-date as we went to press, here's what you can expect.

If there is a character not listed here that you would like to meet you can enquire at City Hall if they will be making any appearances during your visit. Please note not all characters will be available on all of the days.

At Disneyland Park

Main Street and Town Square

Daisy or Friends
Every day from 11:15am to 2:00pm
As you enter the front gates of the park and make your way into Town Square, the spot for Daisy Duck's meet-and-greet is near the entrance to the Discovery Arcade.

Minnie or Friends
Every day 11:00am to 4:00pm
On the other side of Town Square, just next to the entrance to the Liberty Arcade, meet Minnie or one of her Disney friends.

Donald or Friends
Every day 11:00am to 4:00pm
Toward the end of Main Street meet Donald or Friends outside Casey's Corner.

Frontierland

Woody or Friends
Every day 11:00am to 12:15pm and 2:30 to 4:45pm
Meet Woody or his Toy Story pals opposite Cowboy Cookout Barbecue.

Adventureland

Baloo or Friends
Every day 11:15am to 2:15pm
Meet the guys from Jungle Book near the Hakuna Matata restaurant.

Chip and Dale or Friends
Every day 11:15am to 2:30pm
Meet Chip and Dale near Colonel Hathi's Pizza Outpost

Meeting Woody in Frontierland.

Jack Sparrow or Friends
Every day at 11:45am / 12.45pm / 1:45 pm
A brief sighting of Jack Sparrow or his pirate friends at La Plage des Pirates as he mingles among the crowd and poses for photos

Aladdin or Friends
Every day 10:00am to 4:15 pm
Meet Aladdin, Jasmine or maybe Jafar near the Agrabah Café

Fantasyland
Fantasyland is definitely the place to bring your family if you are looking to meet a character or two, as this is the only zone in the park with fixed meet-and-greet opportunities.

Jafar.

Alice or friends
Every day between 11:15am and 2:00pm
Find Alice at the entrance to the Curious Labyrinth for a quick meeting and a photo-shoot opportunity.

Meet Mickey Mouse
Every day 10:00am to 5pm
A fixed meet-and-greet opportunity, Mickey Mouse can be found in his own special theatre, just next to the Disneyland Railroad Fantasyland Station. Join the queue as early as possible in the morning to go backstage and meet the famous magical Mouse himself.

Disney Princesses: A Royal Invitation
Every day 10:00am to 3:30pm
On the other side of Alice's Curious Labyrinth, a fixed meet-and-greet opportunity. If this is top of your to-do list, make sure you get here first thing. Check at City Hall as you enter the front gates of the park if it's important to you to know which princesses are available on your particular day.

Discoveryland

An Encounter with Darth Vader
Every day 10:00am to 5:00pm
Meet the Dark Lord himself near Starport

At Walt Disney Studios

Front Lot

Goofy or Friends
Every day 10:00am to 4:15pm
Meet Goofy and his Disney friends in the Place des Frères Lumière

Toon Studio

Mickey or Friends
Every day 10:00am to 12:15pm and 2:30pm to 3:45 pm
Meet Mickey and his Disney friends in Toon Plaza, to the left
of Crush's Coaster

Buzz Lightyear
Every day 10:00am to 12:15pm
Meet Buzz or some of his friends from Andy's room in Toon
Plaza

Disney Characters
Every day 2:30pm to 3:45pm
Come to Toon Plaza and be surprised by today's character
meet-and-greet. Who knows, perhaps you will meet Remy
from Ratatouille, or Sully from Monsters Inc?

Belle
Every day 11:00am to 3:00 pm
Meet Belle from Beauty and the Beast at the Art of Disney
Animation attraction

Meet Spiderman
Every day 10:00am to 4:30pm
Combine your snack stop with a meeting with one of the most
famous superheroes in the world at the Blockbuster Café.

At a character meal

Auberge de Cendrillon
A real special event – and a pricey one at that – but a meal in
this restaurant will certainly be memorable. You will enjoy a
three-course meal in an elegant setting and meet Suzy and
Perla, Cinderella's mice, as well as some beautiful Disney
Princesses. During the meal, usually three princesses and
their princes will enter and perform two set-piece dances.
They will visit every table to sign autographs, pose for
pictures and chat. Children are encouraged to dress up, and
little girls who happen to be dressed as one of the Princesses
in attendance that day will receive extra special attention. It's
a lovely spectacle, and the food is good quality too. €66 or
€55 adults, €37 or €31 children (see page 94).

Inventions (lunch and dinner)
You can meet the likes of Chip 'n' Dale, Tigger, Mickey, Minnie
and Donald Duck at Inventions Restaurant in Disneyland
Hotel for lunch or dinner (€50 to €60 adults, €25 to €30

children). They also put in an appearance at Sunday Brunch from 1pm to 3pm (€64 adults, €32 children). You don't have to be staying at Disneyland Hotel to participate. (see page 34).

Plaza Gardens Restaurant (breakfast only)
Head to the Plaza Gardens Restaurant in Main Street for an American-style buffet breakfast and you will meet some of your favourite Disney characters such as Mickey, Minnie, Pluto, Chip 'n' Dale and Goofy. There's no guarantee of seeing any specific character as these vary. Wherever these guys appear, you can expect a relaxed, lively, fun atmosphere. Book up to two months in advance (see page 78).

Tips on meeting the characters
- Younger children may find the characters scary as they are larger-than-life. It may be worth seeing their reaction to the characters in the park before booking a character meal.
- Give children time to get used to a character and to approach them at their own pace.
- The 'furry' characters have trouble holding a normal-sized pen and may refuse to sign with one if you're unlucky. You can either buy a chunky biro once you're there, they are readily available in the souvenir shops, or you could take a fat marker pen with you.
- Characters are quite happy to sign autographs or have their photograph taken with adults as well as with children.
- Characters take their role seriously – ask them a question about the movie they are in and they will be happy to tell you all about it.
- Characters always have an assistant with them for safety. The assistants are often willing to take photographs for you if you ask them politely.
- Children dressed up as a character will get more attention given to them than those who aren't.

Dining options
There are a number of different types of restaurant available at Disneyland Paris. Buffet restaurants have a selection of food available at the buffet bar. You can go up as many times as you want and eat as much as you like. Character buffets allow you to meet and interact with the Disney characters appearing that day. Counter service or quick service venues operate in the same way as McDonalds but are often slow due to long queues and poor service. At table- or sit-down

service restaurants you select from the menu at your table and a waiter or waitress comes to take your order.

Most restaurants offer a set menu (prix fixe) usually consisting of a main course, a choice of dessert and a soft drink. At full service restaurants, the cheaper the set menu, the more limited the choice is.

Disney do their best to accommodate those with special dietary requirements, vegetarians and those wanting a slightly healthier option at most restaurants and it's worth asking for these options when you order.

Restaurant reservations

If there is a specific restaurant you would like to eat at, it is worth booking in advance. Restaurants take bookings up to 60 days in advance but you will usually be able to get a table two weeks in advance. To make a reservation phone +33 (0) 1 60 30 40 50 (they speak English). You can also book at any Disney hotel lobby, at City Hall in Disneyland Park or at Studio Services at Walt Disney Studios.

Suitability of rides

Disney use height to gauge whether a child is safe to ride and they strictly adhere to this. However, even if your child is the right height to ride, they may find certain aspects of the ride frightening. Our ratings in the next two chapters show which age group each ride is most suitable for; however, this is a recommendation only – you know your child best. If you're in any doubt, it's a good idea to do the ride first yourself to test its suitability. Most rides are unsuitable for babies under 1 year of age.

Disney also let you know which rides are not suitable for those with back or neck problems, those who suffer from motion sickness and those who are pregnant. We have also included this in the ride information where applicable.

Other useful information

For other practical information such as baby care, disabled guests, French phrases, lockers, lost children, lost property, pushchair (stroller) and wheelchair rental see the quick reference of practical information on pages 151–58.

BRIT TIP

If you are used to the strict height restrictions in place at UK theme parks, you will notice the difference in the number and range of rides at Disneyland Paris on which very young children and even toddlers are permitted. This is great for all the family to enjoy together, once you have taken that moment to assess for yourself if a ride is right for your child.

A ROMANTIC BREAK AT DISNEYLAND PARIS

If you're a fan of Disney's enchanted stories or the magical childhood films, you couldn't find a more romantic place to visit than Disneyland Paris.

Of course, the classic fairy tales depicted all around both parks have their perfect endings, providing a natural backdrop for your own special time, while the whimsical musical accompaniment generates a happy mood and helps to create an atmosphere in which you can suspend reality for a few days and enjoy a little time in your own idyll. It's the ideal place to create some happy memories.

A number of hotels listed in chapter three are perfect for couples who are looking for somewhere quiet, charming and exquisitely romantic. What could be more enchanting than staying at a renovated farmhouse in a peaceful location? The difficulty will be choosing between a rustic-style room with four-poster bed at the Domaine de Bellevue, or the simple elegance of studio accommodation at Domaine de Crecy. Other tranquil retreats include Le Manoir de Gressy, with its distinctive pink shutters and chic décor and Chateau de Sancy, refined and luxurious; both offer an outdoor heated swimming pool, tennis court and gourmet restaurant.

To embrace a traditional royal theme during your stay, book a suite in the Vienna House Dream Castle Hotel. Wander through the French-style gardens and around the nearby lake before returning to your regal room and four-poster bed for the night. For something modern, serene and sophisticated, book a premium room at the Relais Spa Val d'Europe; here you can enjoy some luxury amenities together such as the sunlit indoor pool, sauna and hot tub.

The parks themselves offer plenty of romantic activities. Hop into a classic horse-drawn carriage or streetcar for a short ride down Main Street, or share a seat on one of the galloping horses on Le Carrousel de Lancelot – especially romantic when the lights are switched on after dark. You and your partner can also have fun getting lost in Alice's Curious Labyrinth, have an intimate conversation while you glide across the water on the riverboat cruise at Thunder Mesa Riverboat Landing, or have a go on Big Thunder Mountain after dark and cuddle up in a two-seater car for an exhilarating ride together. Out in Disney Village, enjoy a five-minute fabulous view as you float up in the PanoraMagique hot air balloon.

Take some time out from the noise of the parks and book a couple's massage at one of the Disney or nearby spas in the area. For a surcharge, you and your partner can enjoy a relaxing massage or facial together in the Disneyland Hotel's onsite spa. Here you will find massage beds scattered with rose petals and essential oils, and friendly and expert staff. Alternatively, visit the Asian Villa Spa at the Dream Castle Hotel for sauna, steam room and a whole variety of treatments and massages for you and your loved one to indulge in. Book a relaxing full body massage, a facial or a scrub before lounging in the adult-only indoor pool. During the Christmas season, enjoy ice-skating together on the Hotel New York ice rink.

Whilst visiting Disneyland Paris might be top of your agenda, it would be a shame to miss out on 'the city of love' itself which

overflows with romantic locations. The centre of Paris is only 45 minutes away by RER train direct from Marne-la-Vallee. See the city from the Eiffel Tower at night, stroll through the cobbled streets of Montmartre, home to artists and dancers, or walk hand in hand along the banks of the Seine. Perhaps lesser known is the Place Dauphine, a beautiful square with outdoor cafes and restaurants near the western side of Île de la Cité. It's a great place to linger - at weekends you might see locals playing bocce, a game similar to bowls.

Parisian restaurateurs are renowned for combining fine dining with romantic settings. For a memorable experience, dine in style with your loved one as you cruise down the Seine on an all-glass boat and admire the city lip up at night (€69-€99 per person; scan the QR code for website). Alternatively, take a seat looking down on the city at 58 Tour Eiffel and enjoy soft lighting, a warm ambiance and a 3-course dinner cooked to perfection (€99 per person; scan the QR code for website).

Scan the QR code above for more information about dining whilst cruising down the Seine.

Scan the QR code above for more information about dining at the Eiffel Tower.

If your budget won't quite stretch to that, there are plenty of Parisian restaurants offering food in the region of €20-€40 per person. Le Café du Commerce, close to the Eiffel Tower is a light and airy, multi-level restaurant with classic French décor and bistro-style fare.

Le Hide and L'Etoile 1903, two restaurants near the Arc de Triomphe are perfect for a romantic dinner - reviewers have commented on the wonderful ambience, attentive staff and superb food at both establishments. Montmartre is teeming with romantic venues: Seb'on is 'cosy' with 'outstanding food'; Chez Toinette offers an 'enticing menu and friendly service' and Sacrée Fleur serves 'the best beef I've ever tasted'.

Those on a small budget can reserve a table at Le Procope where Napoleon once dined, or at Le Gourmet for exquisite food at excellent value for money (€18.50 for a three-course meal).

Back at Disneyland Paris, you won't be short of choices for a meal a deux, but - beware! - these are among the most expensive restaurants in the parks. The Blue Lagoon Restaurant in Adventureland is known for its tasty seafood and romantic lighting, although if possible request a table away from the water's edge - while this is a good area to soak up the ambience, the continual passing of boats on the Pirates Of The Caribbean ride will provide a noisy and unwanted distraction. Auberge de Cendrillon in Fantasyland features appearances by the Disney Princes and Princesses, who entertain the diners with set-piece ballroom dances during their three-course meal. Although the Princesses are a magnet for families with young children, the quiet and elegant atmosphere in the restaurant is equally suitable for an intimate dinner for two, you can enjoy dressing for dinner in smart casual wear and the food served is arguably the best you will find in either of the parks although at €75 per head it doesn't come cheap!

Over at the hotels, the Manhattan Restaurant at Hotel New York offers a cool

Central Park look and a refined menu accompanied by classic New York jazz sounds, while the Newport Bay Yacht Club restaurant overlooks Lake Disney and has the feel of an early 20th-century New England club, with its nostalgic photographs and nautical decorations.

When you want to spend time over a drink or two, Café Fantasia in the Disneyland Hotel is an elegant piano bar that serves delicious cocktails, while the Hotel New York has an American-themed setting with similarly ornate drinks. Captain's Quarters in the Newport Bay Club has a large drinks menu including all of the nautical favourites as well as themed cocktails. Arguably the most romantic of all is the Redwood Bar and Lounge at Hotel Sequoia, especially in winter, with its warm and cosy atmosphere around the roaring log fire.

Weddings

Disney now offer a tailored wedding service that allows lucky couples to book their dream wedding day in the park itself or in one of their themed hotels. For many Disney lovers, this is a once in a lifetime chance to have their very own fairy-tale wedding, complete with all the trimmings.

The happy couple have their own Disney wedding planner on hand to make sure their day is picture-perfect. The bride and groom can also choose from the following themed packages or 'Wedding Collections':

Disney's Newport Bay Club
From 32,000 euros

This 1920s-inspired celebration takes place on the shores of the nautical-themed Newport Bay Club hotel, where guests can wine and dine under the sun and overlooking the Disney Lake.

Disneyland Hotel
From 44,000 euros

The next step up in the wedding price range takes place at the Victoriana-inspired Disneyland Hotel right on the doorstep of Disneyland Park. This package has even more Disney-themed trimmings with table settings and a spectacular dining service staged against this classic old-world backdrop.

Castle Courtyard
From 55,000 euros

For an unbeatable Disney wedding experience, the happy couple can also go all the way and opt for a ceremony right next to Sleeping Beauty Castle itself. You can't get much more regal than that for your happy ever after.

The little extras

When talking to your wedding planner about what you want for your special day, there's a whole list of additional services you can request. These may include:

- Live music
- Video and audio equipment
- Personally customisable decorations
- Appearances by Disney characters
- Performances by Disney entertainers

These do come at an additional charge and are subject to change based on availability and season. For more information about planning a Disneyland Paris wedding, email their service at **dlp.weddings@disney.com**

6 Disneyland Park

With five intricately detailed magical lands to explore and the towering blue-roofed turrets of the Sleeping Beauty Castle forming its centrepiece, the Disneyland Park is truly the heart of this European experience.

Whether you find yourself surrounded by the futuristic neon lights of Discoveryland; in the Wild West of Frontierland; in the exotic unchartered territory of Adventureland, or in the fairy-tale dreamscape of Fantasyland – entering any of these areas is like becoming Alice herself and falling down the rabbit hole into an alternative reality.

The Disneyland Park opened in April 1992 as the first Disney theme park in Europe. Structured in a similar way to the Magic Kingdom in Walt Disney World Orlando, it brought the style, flavour and many of the attractions of that park to within easy reach of the European audience. The more compact Walt Disney Studios followed alongside in later years.

Although claiming to have enough to delight fans from age two to 92, it is certainly true that the majority of the rides and attractions in the Disneyland Park are family friendly. Thrill-seekers used to the adrenaline rush on offer in Orlando may be slightly disappointed by the limited number of high-octane rides in the Disneyland Park, although the sister park, Walt Disney Studios, has more to offer on these lines. **Star Wars Hyperspace Mountain** (previously **Space Mountain: Mission 2**) is really the only ride for serious thrill-seekers and is a popular favourite for its pitch-black twists and turns and its high-speed launch tunnel. The **Big Thunder Mountain** and **Indiana Jones and the Temple of Peril** rollercoasters are the only other 'big' rides in the park, although the newly opened **Star Tours: The Adventure Continues**, while being a motion simulator rather than a rollercoaster, is exciting enough to delight most riders.

Character meet-and-greets are a big part of the attraction in the Disneyland Park. Fixed locations for character meetings include the Princess Pavilion, which welcomes guests for royal visits with the Disney Princesses, while Mickey Mouse offers a photo-shoot opportunity in his theatre dressing room. The daily programme (see pages 59–61) contains full details of the times and locations for the other character meet-and-greet opportunities throughout the park.

At mealtimes, the offerings available across the park range from the basic quick-fix hot-dog stands and counter service fast-food eateries to full, licensed sit-down restaurants. There is a good, wide choice of menus, themed to fit in with the land in which they are situated: the **Lucky Nugget Saloon** offering a Tex-Mex buffet in Frontierland, or the **Agrabah Cafe** offering couscous and shwarma chicken and lamb in Adventureland, for instance. However, the food quality can be disappointing, especially at the counter-service restaurants, and it is certainly not cheap.

Refurbishments

Many of the park's most popular rides go through their annual renovations during the quieter 'off-peak' periods. This means that the likes of **Big Thunder Mountain, Star Wars Hyperspace Mountain, Pirates of the Caribbean, Peter Pan's Flight** and many others can be out of order for weeks at a time during winter. This was especially the case during the run up to the 25th anniversary celebrations, as the park had perhaps become slightly dishevelled over the years and was in need of some renovation and the glittering lick of fresh paint it has now received under the scheme called 'Experience Enhancement Plan' (EEP).

With EEP completed in time for the 25th Anniversary celebrations, further renovations should be at a minimum for the next year or so, especially in comparison with the disruption experienced during the 2015–16 overhaul. However, it is still worth keeping an eye out for any closures or refurbishments that might be taking place during your planned visit through the Disneyland Paris website. Scan the QR code for the latest news.

Scan the QR code above for current and scheduled refurbishments.

Main Street USA

Enter the front gates of the park and you will immediately find yourself on the central boulevard of a Midwest American town, bustling from the industrial boom of the 1910s. Main Street USA is mostly a shopping area that includes the famous Emporium, modelled on a Victorian department store, offering unique souvenirs and collectors' items. There are also clothing shops, a bookshop and even a real barber shop – Dapper Dans.

Along Main Street there are a good number of cafes and restaurants to choose from as well as two Victorian-themed arcades, drawing you back into a golden age of technology and industry.

Town Square 3

Once you have passed through the ornate arches of the Disneyland Railroad Station and through the gates, you will immediately enter the Town Square. This quaint area features a small central bandstand and a surrounding selection of flowerbeds, trees and streetlamps to lend it an authentic atmosphere.

Scan the QR code above for an online map of Disneyland Park.

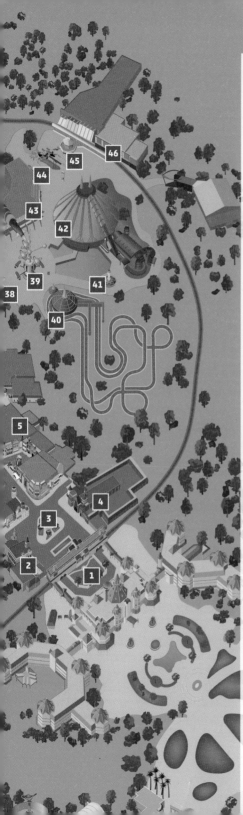

Disneyland Park

A list rides | **B list** rides

Main Street USA

1 Main Street Railroad Station
2 City Hall
3 Town Square
4 Main Street Transportation Company
5 Discovery Arcade
6 Liberty Arcade
7 Central Plaza

Frontierland

8 **Phanton Manor**
9 Thunder Mesa Riverboat Landing
10 Rustler Roundup Shootin' Gallery
11 **Big Thunder Mountain**
12 Pocahontas Indian Village
13 Chaparral Theatre
14 Frontierland Railroad Station
15 Fort Comstock

Adventureland

16 Le Passage Enchanté d'Aladdin
17 La Plage de Pirates
18 La Cabane des Robinson
19 **Indiana Jones and the Temple of Peril**
20 Adventure Isle
21 Skull Rock and Pirate Galleon
22 **Pirates of the Caribbean**

Fantasyland

23 **Sleeping Beauty Castle**
24 Les voyages de Pinocchio
25 Blanche-Neige et les Sept Nains
26 Le Carrousel de Lancelot
27 Dumbo the Flying Elephant
28 **Peter Pan's Flight**
29 **Meet Mickey Mouse**
30 Fantasyland Railroad Station
31 Alice's Curious Labyrinth
32 Mad Hatter's Tea Cups
33 Casey Jr – le Petit Train du Cirque
34 Le Pays des Contes de Fées
35 **Princess Pavilion**
36 'it's a small world'
37 Royal Castle Stage

Discoveryland

38 **Buzz Lightyear Laser Blast**
39 Orbitron – Machines Volantes
40 Autopia
41 Les Mystères du Nautilus
42 **Star Wars Hyperspace Mountain**
43 Jedi Training Academy
44 Arcade Beta
45 **Star Tours: The Adventures Continue**
46 Discoveryland Railroad Station

City Hall

City Hall

City Hall is located on the left of Town Square and acts as the tourism and information office for this park. This is the place to go if you need any of the following services:

- Currency Exchange
- Lost and found
- Restaurant reservations
- Lost children in the park
- General park information, maps and guides
- Providing feedback, complaints or asking any questions you might have

The City Hall provides a selection of multi-lingual Cast Members (staff) to cater to your needs.

Discovery and Liberty Arcades 5 6

On either side of Town Square, and running along the length of the central boulevard, are two covered walkways. Discovery Arcade, with its Victorian-style gas lamps is elegantly-themed with display cases and images featuring early breakthroughs in human innovation, whilst Liberty Arcade reveals the story behind the Statue of Liberty. Both arcades offer an alternative entrance into all of the shops on the boulevard.

BRIT TIP ☑

If the weather is bad or the pavements are crowded, nip into one of the **arcades**. You can walk the length of the street under cover and away from much of the hustle and bustle. It's not so easy if you have a pushchair, although at quieter times it might still be worth it.

Disneyland Railroad 1 14 30 46

- *20-minute train ride*
- *Any age*

Main Street Transportation

Hop on one of the authentic steam-powered trains at Main Street Station and you can start your visit to the park with a full tour taking you through all the individual lands in the park. On your first visit, this is a great way to get an idea of the theme and style of each of the areas. The trains also stop in Frontierland, Fantasyland and Discoveryland, offering you an alternative way to navigate the park without having to wade through the crowds, or as a means of transport when little ones get too tired to walk.

Main Street Transportation 4

- *5-minute vehicle ride*
- *Any age*

Take a ride on one of the turn-of-the-century motor vehicles parading up and down Main Street, with a selection of five different types of iconic car to choose from: the Fire Engine, the Omnibus, the Limousine, the Mercer and the Paddy Wagon.

For an even more classic form of transport, guests can hop on to the back of one of the horse-drawn streetcars. This may not be the quickest or most efficient mode of transport to get you to the next area on your list, but it offers a unique perk that kids of all ages seem to love.

Dining

Walt's – an American Restaurant

- *€€€ - Highly priced*
- *Table Service*
- *TripAdvisor rating: 4*

Away from the fast-food distributors scattered about Disneyland Paris, this sophisticated restaurant takes American cuisine to the next level – for an additional price. Previous guests have heralded this eatery as 'great for special occasions' with its 'elegant and quiet' atmosphere and high quality food. You can choose a table in one of the six themed rooms, whether you want to sit under the gothic buttresses of the Fantasyland room or are looking to browse the illustrations adorning the Discoveryland room – there is a spot to suit every family. A set menu including starter and main course will set you back around €31, whilst the children's menu including starter, main, dessert and drink costs around €17.

BRIT TIP

The queue at **Main Street station** during peak-season is usually long, 45 minutes on average. At first glance, the queues at other stations look comparatively short – but be aware that most people who get on at Main Street do the full circuit so not many seats become free when the train stops, while at Main Street the whole train empties. It is possible to end up waiting longer for your turn at the other stations than you would at Main Street for this reason.

Book in advance (essential) either through the Dining Reservation Service on +33 1 60 30 40 50 or at the reception desk of your Disney hotel.

Market House Deli

- *€ - Low priced*
- *Quick counter service*
- *TripAdvisor rating: 3.5*

Across from Walt's fine dining experience, you can pick up a pastry, wrap or sandwich from the Market House Deli for a fraction of the price of Walt's. Sandwiches of various fillings cost around €7, whilst desserts and drinks fall under the €4 mark, making it a 'great place to get a quick bite to eat' without breaking your budget.

The Coffee Grinder

- *€ - Low priced*
- *Quick counter service*
- *TripAdvisor rating: 3*

Be warned: reviews of Disneyland Paris coffee in general have not raved about the quality. However, this does not mean that this establishment is any less of a welcome place to take a break from the buzz of the boulevard. Visitors have mentioned that this little pit-stop coffee provider also offers an excellent selection of cakes to have with your beverage, at around €3 or €4 per snack.

The Ice Cream Company

- *€ - Low priced*
- *Quick counter service*
- *TripAdvisor: 4*

The Ice Cream Company is one of the most highly rated ice cream parlours in the parks, serving 'plenty of ice cream flavours and toppings' for around €3 or €4. With popularity, however, come long queues, which an increased number of staff has done little to tackle over the past few years.

Cookie Kitchen

- *€ - Low priced*
- *Quick counter service*
- *TripAdvisor: 3.5*

Many families return to the Cookie Kitchen time and time again as a 'perfect stop off to refuel' whilst at the parks, stocking up on the coffee, hot chocolate and the selection of cookies, croissants, cakes and muffins available. These are priced from around €2 to €4.

BRIT TIP ☑

Main Street outside **Cookie Kitchen** or the **Ice Cream Company** is an excellent little spot in which to stand and watch the daily Parade go by, which means you won't miss any of the action whilst picking up your much-needed snacks.

Cable Car Bake Shop

Cable Car Bake Shop

- ■ *€ - Low priced*
- ■ *Quick counter service*
- ■ *TripAdvisor: 4*

Take a seat in a softly lit booth to hide from the noise of the parks in yet another coffee and cake shop on Main Street. It may not boast much variety in the snack department in comparison to the other similar cafes next door, but the themed setting and honky tonk piano tunes create a fun atmosphere for your afternoon refuelling stop. Prices are reasonable too with a baguette costing around €7 and a cake or pie €4.

Casey's Corner

- ■ *€ - Low priced*
- ■ *Quick counter service*
- ■ *TripAdvisor: 3*

This baseball-themed quick-service eatery provides a welcome savoury break from the sweets and treats of the other cafes on Main Street. Serving classic hot dogs ranging from around €7 on their own to €14 or €15 in a set menu, this is as cheap as lunch options come in Disneyland Paris, even if it isn't the healthiest of choices. Casey's Corner has been given some negative reviews in the past for being 'crowded', 'busy' and a little 'overpriced', but most guests agree you get a tasty hot dog here.

The Gibson Girl Ice Cream Parlour

- ■ *€ - Low priced*
- ■ *Quick counter service*
- ■ *TripAdvisor: 3.5*

Changes have been made to this cute little ice cream parlour over the years, sadly altering its service from a scoop-by-scoop approach to a less value-for-money, by-the-pot distribution system. However, this is still an excellent little pastel-coloured spot to taste the various unique and delicious flavours of Ben & Jerry's ice cream that we know and love so well.

Victoria's Home-style Restaurant

Victoria's Home-Style Restaurant

- €€ - *Mid priced*
- *Quick counter service*
- *TripAdvisor: 2.5*

Based on the design of a 1920s American boarding house, this homely eatery offers a quick, alternative lunchtime option without a high price tag. Many previous visitors have mentioned the 'poor and slow' service and the 'limited menu', but with a set menu of around €12 to €15 per head, this restaurant is perfectly priced and placed for a fuss-free, midday bite to eat.

Plaza Gardens Restaurant

- €€€ - *Highly priced*
- *Buffet service*
- *TripAdvisor: 4*

This buffet option provides a selection of freshly cooked international dishes inside the facade of an elegantly decorated, Victorian leisure pavilion. For under €35 per adult, and for around €17 per child, guests have a wide selection of all-you-can-eat foods available. Reviews have focused on the slightly terse and impolite waiting staff, but mostly all is forgiven in light of the opulent surroundings, velvet curtains and glittering atmosphere of a bygone era.

In spring 2017, the character meals on offer at Café Mickey in the Disney Village were closed and a brand-new character buffet breakfast was opened here at Plaza Gardens. Mickey, Minnie or any of their Disney pals visit tables to sign autographs, pose for pictures and interact with kids, making this a great way to see the characters up-close without the long queues at the meet-and-greet venues. Booking for a character breakfast is essential, but the Plaza Gardens is popular at any time so make sure you reserve a table through the Dining Reservation Service on +33 1 60 30 40 50 or at the reception desk of your Disney Hotel.

Central Plaza 7

At the end of the short yet busy boulevard the path opens out into the Central Plaza: a circular space right in front of the Sleeping Beauty Castle. Main Street Vehicles and Horse Drawn Street Cars will drop you off here after your brief ride.

Central Plaza is the heart of the park: from here there are four paths leading off into the four 'lands'. It is worth getting here before park opening and already knowing which area you

PARK TACTICS

Disneyland Park covers a large area of 140 acres – just over twice the size of Walt Disney Studios. Take this into account when planning your day and bring or hire a pushchair for any younger members of your family. Even if they are old enough to walk, it will be very hard for them to walk all day.

Download the official Disneyland Paris app on either a smart-phone or an iPad. This will give you updates on the waiting times for certain rides, the opening times of different cafes and restaurants, and you can easily find out where the meeting points are for various characters.

Queues are at their shortest in the first two and last two hours of the day, so try to plan your day around this. Do as many of the popular attractions as possible early in the morning before using the FastPass system during the busier hours.

If your children are keen to experience a royal meeting with one of their favourite characters at the Princess Pavilion make your way to this attraction first as you will need to take a timed slot and these sell out early in the day.

Rides and attractions are often quieter during the parade that takes place at 5:30pm, so if you have already seen this dazzling display on another day this is a prime time to skip a lengthy wait.

want to explore first so you can position yourself at the correct entrance ready to move when the cast members drop the rope.

Central Plaza is also a viewing area for the daily Disney Stars on Parade show and the nightly Disney Illuminations fireworks, light projection and special effects show, so make sure you scout out a good viewing spot well in advance.

Frontierland

As you step through the surrounding trees and under the wooden gates you will find yourself back on the frontier with the original American pioneers, daring it all in the Wild West. The large central mound of **Big Thunder Mountain** – with its famous high thrills roller coaster and surrounding lake – rises above a busy town of steakhouses, shooting ranges and lively saloons, while **Phantom Manor** looms on the hill as an unmissable spooky attraction.

Fort Comstock 15

- Walk through attraction
- Any age

Directly as you enter Frontierland you see the building facades of American Old West, and you can climb up to the ramparts to enjoy the period detail in the building and a view

BRIT TIP

Make your way to **Big Thunder Mountain** first to beat the queues or grab a FastPass. During high season and at peak times of the day – between 12pm and 4pm – the wait can be as much as two hours long and FastPasses are often gone well before lunchtime.

over Frontierland. This attraction can provide a little welcome peace for adults while the little ones are busy elsewhere – although kids will enjoy climbing the ramparts too.

BRIT TIP

Try going to the **Rustler Roundup Shootin' Gallery** at the end of the day as it gets dark: not only are there fewer people around, but the lights also make it easier to see and take aim.

Rustler Roundup Shootin' Gallery 🔟

- *Age 8+*

Try your hand at this Wild West-themed shooting gallery to win both the admiration of your family and potentially a prize. Guests are presented with moving targets, cacti obstructions, characters from the frontier and multiple special effects to push the shooter to their limits. This is one of the only attractions that entail a surcharge in the park – alongside Dapper Dan's haircuts and shaves and the gaming arcades in Discoveryland – although this has not taken away from its overall popularity.

Thunder Mesa Riverboat Landing 9️

- *15-minute riverboat cruise*
- *Any age*
- *Average wait times less than 30 minutes*

BRIT TIP

Phantom Manor is a good place to come if the weather takes a turn for the worse as the waiting area is covered and the attraction itself is all indoors.

Two paddleboats, based on 19th-century designs, take guests around Big Thunder Mountain and past waterfalls and plush trees on this 15-minute ride. This water-bound tour of Frontierland is an excellent way of viewing the area from a different perspective and at a leisurely pace, but it can become crowded and popular during the summer months. Note that this ride closes early, usually around 7pm.

Phantom Manor 8️

- *7-minute dark narrative cart ride*
- *Age 8+; may frighten little ones*
- *Average wait times up to 30 minutes*

This dark narrative ride through the haunted bowels of this Colonial mansion provides an excellent change from the surrounding Wild West-themed attractions. Guests of age 5 and above can try the ride if they don't find the prospect of ghosts, ghouls and skeletons too frightening, as this is truly one of the park's most modern and thrilling narrative cart rides. The special effects are far superior to those shown in either Blanche-Neige et les Sept Nains or Les Voyages de Pinocchio (both being older, more traditional narrative cart rides) over in Fantasyland and the attention to detail is stunning. Look out for the picture of Walt Disney himself on a table in the Manor!

Thunder Mesa Riverboats

*Taking the plunge on Big
Thunder Mountain*

Big Thunder Mountain 11

- 4-minute big thrill coaster ride
- Fastpass
- On-ride photo
- Minimum height of 1.02m
- Age 8+; may frighten little ones
- Not suitable for pregnant women or those with heart,
  back or neck problems
- Average wait times 90 to 120 minutes

This is probably the most family-friendly roller coaster in
Disneyland Paris, with a top speed of around 50kmph and
no inversions. It could reasonably be described as a classic
'old school' rollercoaster of the type that many ages enjoy.
However, some younger children might become frightened
in the darker sections of this ride, as the runaway mine
carts hurtle through bat-infested caves and dark tunnels.
Unlike equivalent rides at other Disney locations, this
version is unique in that it is positioned on a towering island
surrounded by a lake. Explosions, waterfalls and spectacular
scenery add to a truly memorable ride experience.

Pocahontas Indian Village 12

- Playground and picnic area
- Any age; fun for little ones

Around the back of Big Thunder Mountain you can find a
peaceful Native American camp on the banks of the lake,
where a playground sits amongst the trees for your family
to enjoy. This area is perfect for younger kids, or as a place to
bring your lunch on a sunny day, away from the bustle of the
shops and cafés.

BRIT TIP ☑

The carts at the back
of the **Big Thunder
Mountain** experience
the most momentum
and you feel the speed
most seated here. Ask
to move forward or
wait for the next ride if
you are shown to the
back and you know you
won't enjoy it – or if you
have young children. At
quiet times of year, you
may be able to request
a seat at the back on the
next ride if you want the
biggest thrill.

Pocahontas Indian Village

BRIT TIP ☑

The **Chaparral Theatre** was renovated a few years ago to include a roof over the audience, which is great in bad weather. This, however, means that there are a couple of obstructing pillars in the way of certain seats on both the left and the right of the theatre, so arrive around 20 minutes before the start of the show to bag a prime viewing spot.

Chaparral Theatre 🔟

- *Covered theatre*
- *20-minute show: The Forest of Enchantment*

A fixed theatre venue where a variety of song and dance shows have been held over the years. The show for 2017 was The Forest of Enchantment: A Disney musical adventure (see page 100). Given its popularity, it is highly likely this will return at some point in 2018.

Dining

The Lucky Nugget Saloon

- *€ - Low priced*
- *Quick counter service*
- *TripAdvisor rating: 3.5*

Across the pathway from the Thunder Mesa Mercantile Building, the Lucky Nugget Saloon immediately catches your eye. Previous guests have mentioned the true 'western atmosphere' to be found at this eatery, as well as reasonable prices allowing each person to pay less than €20 for a main, dessert and unlimited soft drinks. The Lucky Nugget even has a live band playing regularly to provide guests with authentic American entertainment.

Last Chance Café

- *€ - Low priced*
- *Quick counter service*
- *TripAdvisor rating: 3.5*

Last Chance Café offers 'excellent quick service' and cheap 'tasty food' according to reviewers. With dishes not even pushing past the €15 mark, you really can eat on a budget at this small Old West outpost, which is adorned with Wanted posters, holsters and saddles from all the other mischief-makers who have been and gone before.

Last Chance Café

Silver Spur Steakhouse
- €€ - *Moderately priced*
- *Table service*
- *TripAdvisor rating: 3.5*

The Silver Spur Steakhouse offers a sit-down meal of American and Tex-Mex cuisine for moderate to high prices. Set menus of a starter, main course and dessert set you back around €37 per person, although there are also main courses on offer for between €20 and €25. Visitors to this eatery have been happy with the large portions, the impressive children's menu and the live music which provides a unique and welcoming experience.

Reserve your table in advance either through the Dining Reservation Service on +33 1 60 30 40 50 or at the Reception Desk of your Disney Hotel.

Fuente del Oro Restaurante
- € - *Low priced*
- *Quick counter service*
- *TripAdvisor rating: 3*

Reviews for this Mexican-cuisine establishment have raved about the 'quick service' and the 'absolutely scrumptious' dishes to try here. In offering a menu that provides something other than burgers and chicken nuggets in this fast food-heavy theme park, the Fuente del Oro Restaurante brings Mexican colour and flavour into this small corner of Frontierland. There are a number of set menus ranging from around €12 to €15 or you can choose from a range of a la carte dishes such as chicken taco salad, chicken fajitas or chicken and beef tacos.

Cowboy Cookout Barbecue
- € - *Low priced*
- *Quick counter service*
- *TripAdvisor rating: 4*

Located across the water from Big Thunder Mountain and just next to the Pocahontas Indian Village on the outer edge of Frontierland, the Cowboy Cookout Barbecue is a great eatery for any time of the year. During the winter, escape from the cold and damp by sitting next to the open roaring fires. Even in the height of summer, who could say no to well-priced barbecue food with the possibility of accompanying live music? This is also an excellent place to escape the throng of the crowds during the daily parade. There are three set menus from around €12 to €14 and various a la carte dishes from around €7 to €12.

BRIT TIP

The flame-grills used in the kitchens make the air in the **Silver Spur** quite smoky. Great for authentic Old West atmosphere – a little hard on the eyes after a while!

Adventureland

Step through the gates from Central Plaza and you will enter an exotic world in a remote, foreign land. The sheer patchwork of different cultures represented in this land can become a little confusing at times, but nothing in the parks can really match the awesome scenery that makes up the Pirate Beach, the Galleon, and the small shopping area transformed into the marketplace of Aladdin's Agrabah.

The main access from Central Plaza is not the only way into Adventureland. Walk through Frontierland past **Big Thunder Mountain** on your left and keep going to the far end of the land. Follow one of a number of interconnected paths for a shortcut straight into Adventureland. There are several points along the paths where you can get a lovely photo of the Castle too; it'll be from a side view but it's none the worse for that and it won't have the crowds of people in the background which are inescapable in the traditional front-on pictures taken from Main Street.

Le Passage Enchanté d'Aladdin

Le Passage Enchanté d'Aladdin 16

- *Covered walkthrough*
- *Any age*

In comparison to the submarine-themed **Les Mystères du Nautilus** over in Discoveryland, this covered walkthrough attraction can seem a little on the small side. However, this cute passage can be fun for *Aladdin*-lovers of any age with its displays of miniatures scenes from the film and its warm magical glow away from the hustle and bustle of the Agrabah market.

La Cabane des Robinson 18

- *Elevated walkthrough adventure*
- *Any age*

After the success of a similar attraction in both the California and Orlando parks, Disneyland Paris created its own version of the Robinson Family tree house. Guests can wander up the stairs and wooden walkways through the home of this castaway family, where they will find bedrooms, a kitchen, a library and some excellent views out across Adventureland.

La Plage de Pirates 17

- *Pirate-themed playgrounds*
- *Age: under 9s*
- *Maximum height 1.40m*

With a selection of slides, rope ladders and plenty of pirate-themed climbing apparatus, this is a fun-filled corner of Adventureland. Bring your family here for a bit of downtime and some outdoor activity after lunch.

Adventure Isle 20

■ *Exploration area*

■ *Any age*

This exotic maze of plant life and rocky jungle paths is a great way to escape from the theme park machinery and fast-food outlets. With rope suspension bridges and dark, gloomy caves for your family to trek through, you can while away the time in the great outdoors looking for some hidden treasures. Stay together as a family though; some of these walkways can be slippery for younger and less stable visitors. Following recent renovations, the rock work has been reshaped and repainted and many of the waterfalls are now fully functioning again.

Pirate Galleon 21

■ *Exploration area*

■ *Any age*

Jump aboard Captain's Hook's famous pirate galleon to explore the deck of this iconic vessel. At certain times there are even Disney actors playing pirates on deck to get you and your family shipshape as you learn the ropes and look around this authentic-looking replica.

Pirates of the Caribbean 22

■ *10-minute dark narrative boat ride*

■ *Guests may get splashed*

■ *Any age*

■ *Average wait times 15 to 45 minutes*

Another much-loved ride in the Disneyland Park, this has benefitted from a big renovation for the 25th Anniversary. **Pirates of the Caribbean** reopened in July 2017 with the inclusion of Jack Sparrow animatronics to tie in with the film series and plus an animatronic Captain Barbossa and images of Davy Jones and Blackbeard. The boats move through huge caverns showing scenes from lawless pirate-run towns, including furious fights, and through glittering caves of gold and jewels. As part of the recent renovation, an original scene depicting women being auctioned to the pirates was remade into an auction of loot. Two short plunges during the ride add a small splash and plenty of fun to the adventure.

BRIT TIP

If you aren't looking to see the parade, the **Pirate's Beach playground** is a good place to get away from the crowds.

Pirate Galleon

BRIT TIP

The queue area for **Pirates of the Caribbean** is almost as good as the ride itself, such is the level of detail in the design. Enjoy the time browsing the all the little pirate-themed nuances and the queue might almost seem not long enough!

*Indiana Jones and the
Temple of Peril*

Indiana Jones and the Temple of Peril

- *2-minutes 10 seconds big thrill outdoor coaster ride*
- *Fastpass*
- *Minimum height: 1.40m*
- *Age 8+*
- *Not suitable for under 8s, pregnant women or those with heart, back or neck problems*
- *Average wait times 30 to 60 minutes*

If the Big Thunder Mountain mine cart ride didn't quite thrill you enough, then the **Indiana Jones and the Temple of Peril** roller coaster might fit the bill. Step into another mine cart and strap yourself in for a fast and furious ride around a crumbling temple. With multiple twists and turns and a full inversion, the ride is over before you know it, and you will find yourself back in the long queue once again, raring for another go. As rollercoasters go, this one feels quite rickety and shaky in places so check the restrictions before you get in the queue. It would be a very bad idea for anyone with a bad back to ride.

Dining

Restaurant Agrabah Café

- *€€ - Moderately priced*
- *Buffet service*
- *TripAdvisor rating: 3.5*

For around €35 per adult and €20 per child, you can taste the worldly delights of this all-you-can-eat Mediterranean, Moroccan and Middle Eastern buffet in the heart of Agrabah. Bear in mind that past reviews have been quite varied, with many heralding this eatery as an 'interesting good buffet', while others comment on the poor variety and selection of dishes. Reserve your table in advance either through the Dining Reservation Service on +33 1 60 30 40 50 or at the Reception Desk of your Disneyland Hotel.

Blue Lagoon Restaurant

- ■ €€€ - Highly priced
- ■ Table service
- ■ TripAdvisor rating: 3.5

This restaurant provides a unique moonlit dining experience, no matter what time of day it actually is. If you don't mind the higher prices – you can expect to spend up to €40 per person – then this seafood eatery perched on the banks of a mermaid lagoon could be a great choice for a special one-off meal. The Pirates of the Caribbean ride passes right beside the terraced restaurant seating area so you can watch and wave as the boats go by, a favourite with young children.

Reserve your table in advance either through the Dining Reservation Service on +33 1 60 30 40 50 or at the Reception Desk of your Disneyland Hotel.

Colonel Hathi's Pizza Outpost

- ■ € - Low priced
- ■ Quick counter service
- ■ TripAdvisor rating: 3.5

A little bizarrely, this British Colonial-style clubhouse serves Italian cuisine for its guests although the sheer numbers of happy previous customers don't seem to be complaining! One review mentioned that this Jungle Book-themed eatery was 'one of the better fast food' places to be found throughout the entirety of Disneyland Paris, offering set menus of a main, dessert and a drink for less than €15 per head.

Colonel Hathi's Pizza Outpost.

Restaurant Hakuna Matata

- ■ € - Moderately priced
- ■ Quick counter service
- ■ TripAdvisor rating: 4

This fast food provider themed on The Lion King is another favourite with previous guests, who seem completely taken by the warm, 'lovely atmosphere' and the spicy main courses on offer. Visitors can once again pick up a set menu – including a main, a dessert and a drink – for less than €15, before sitting inside this mud-walled hut and eating lunch with the infamous film soundtrack playing around you.

Restaurant Hakuna Matata.

BRIT TIP ☑

Try to get to the **Princess Pavilion,** then **Dumbo the Flying Elephant** and **Peter Pan** as soon as you can after entering Fantasyland.

Fantasyland

"What youngster has not dreamed of flying with Peter Pan over moonlit London, or tumbling into Alice's nonsensical Wonderland? In Fantasyland, these classic stories of everyone's youth have become realities for youngsters – of all ages – to participate in."

When Walt Disney himself uttered these words he was presenting the idea for Fantasyland in Disneyland Park, California but as the Paris equivalent is heavily based upon the same model, they are no less appropriate here. Through the arches of Sleeping Beauty Castle, guests enter the world of the Disney classic fairytales, whether this means wandering through Alice's Curious Labyrinth, learning the tale of a toy who wants to be a real boy, or meeting those iconic Disney Princesses.

Sleeping Beauty Castle 23

There surely isn't a better entrance to this fairy-tale land than by walking under the arches of the Sleeping Beauty Castle itself. The 167-foot towering castle faithfully represents the classic Disney image as well as including some special aspects of European architecture to make it unique to this Paris park alone. Make sure you look up to take in all of the ornate and elegant details such as the stained glass windows, the chandeliers inside and the pillars sculpted to look like climbing trees reaching up to the ceiling. In the evening, the castle forms the centrepiece to the brand-new and fabulous **Disney Illuminations** firework and light show.

La Tanière du Dragon 23

- ■ *Walkthrough attraction*
- ■ *Age 5+; may frighten very little ones*

To the left of the bridge to the Sleeping Beauty Castle, you can find the small yet spooky **La Tanière du Dragon** (the dragon's lair). This walkthrough amusement takes you down underneath the castle and into the dark dungeons to see the slumbering monstrous beast – be warned, this may frighten some of the youngest members of your family.

La Tanière du Dragon

Sleeping Beauty Castle

La Galerie de la Belle au Bois Dormant 23

- *Walkthrough attraction*
- *Any age*

Once inside the **Sleeping Beauty Castle**, take a left turn up the stairs in the footsteps of Prince Phillip himself as he rushes to Aurora's bedside. Turn left at the top of the stairs to continue around the circular, lavishly decorated gallery before emerging out of the wooden door and on to the balcony. From here you have a perfect viewing spot over Fantasyland, and can easily plan your route to your next destination from this elevated point. There is a lift for pushchairs and disabled access.

Blanche-Neige et les Sept Nains 25

- *2-minute dark narrative cart ride*
- *Age 5+; may frighten little ones*
- *Average wait times 20 to 45 minutes*

Hop into one of the waiting mine carts and start the journey through the story of *Snow White and the Seven Dwarves*. Dramatic lighting, special effects and moving puppetry brings this classic story to life before your very eyes, but make sure all of the younger members of your family are prepared for some of the darker moments in the narrative. It is surprisingly sinister for little ones, and the Evil Queen likes to make an appearance when you least expect it!

Les Voyages de Pinocchio 24

- *2-minute dark narrative cart ride*
- *Age 5+; may frighten little ones*
- *Average wait times 20 to 45 minutes*

Les Voyages de Pinocchio gives guests another opportunity to take a ride through one of Disney's older classic tales. From Geppetto's workshop, follow Pinocchio's journey with his best friend Jiminy Cricket through thick and thin on his quest to become a real boy. Again, certain moments in this ride can prove a bit dark and frightening for younger children, less so than Snow White, but it may still be best to prepare those of a sensitive nature. Overall this is one of the most-loved classic Disney rides in the park.

Le Carrousel de Lancelot 26

- *2-minute carousel ride*
- *Any age*
- *Average wait times under 20 minutes*

BRIT TIP ☑

Le Carrousel de Lancelot can be fun to save for those later hours when it is dark, as it is illuminated with atmospheric, glowing lights.

Take a seat in the horse's saddle for a trip on the merry-go-round located between the Sleeping Beauty Castle and Dumbo the Flying Elephant. At peak times it will be busy, so to minimise the wait you could aim to get in the queue either in the first or last two hours of the day or during the parade – but if that doesn't suit you don't worry too much as the ride loads a large number of people in one go and each ride only lasts 2 minutes so what seems at first like a static never-ending queue does soon dissipate. This is a delightful ride for toddlers, especially as you can ride on the same horse with them (a practice that many UK theme parks have ended for health and safety reasons).

Dumbo the Flying Elephant 27

- *1-minute 30 seconds aerial carousel*
- *Not suitable for children under 1 year of age*
- *Average wait times 60 to 90 minutes*

Dumbo the Flying Elephant

Flying elephants of all colours take to the skies in this aerial carousel, as the Dumbo-shaped carts circle the circus big top for a thrilling, yet gentle adventure. The small joy-stick in every cart allows the riders to decide how high they want to fly, giving you the opportunity to get one of the best panoramic views of Fantasyland and beyond. A thrilling ride for toddlers and young children. Unfortunately, due to its popularity and slow loading, queues can be extremely long at peak times so get here either before 12pm or after 5pm. If you are staying in a Disney hotel, this is an ideal ride to check out during your Extra Magic Hours.

Peter Pan's Flight `28`

- ■ *3-minute dark narrative suspended cart ride*
- ■ *FastPass*
- ■ *Any age*
- ■ *Average wait times 60 to 90 minutes*

Given the number of narrative rides in Fantasyland, it might seem like **Peter Pan's Flight** is one too many. However, this attraction has the added benefit of suspending its visitors in magical flying galleons as they race over the night-time London sky and head for an adventure in Neverland. Grab a FastPass or make your way here first thing in the morning to beat the queues, as this is yet another ride that attracts the masses during those peak hours of the summer season.

Peter Pan's Flight

Alice's Curious Labyrinth `31`

- ■ *10 to 20 minutes walkthrough hedge maze*
- ■ *Any age*
- ■ *No wait time*

If you are visiting the parks during summer, this outdoor hedge maze is the perfect addition to any fun-filled, sunny day. Enter the winding labyrinth and meet the likes of the Cheshire Cat, the Queen of Hearts and the bumbling card soldiers as you try to make your way to the castle at the centre. Dodge the fun water jets which squirt through the hedges when you least expect it! Even if this outdoor activity is not as appealing during the colder winter months, it is all worth it for the view to be had from the top of the castle.

Alice's Curious Labyrinth

BRIT TIP ☑

Casey Jr – le Petit Train du Cirque, **Le Pays des Contes de Fées** and sometimes **Alice's Curious Labyrinth** usually close early, even in peak season.

Mad Hatter's Tea Cups `32`

- ■ *2-minute classic teacup-carousel ride*
- ■ *Any age*
- ■ *Average wait times under 30 minutes*

Climb into a teacup and take a whirl beneath an attractive petal-shaped roof and hanging Japanese lanterns. Each teacup spins in the opposite direction to the rotation of the carousel but if getting dizzy isn't your thing, the wheel inside your teacup enables you to slow down your spin. This is a popular ride so you may prefer to leave it until the end of the day when you will benefit from much shorter queues as well as riding beneath the soft glow of the lanterns. Like

Mad Hatter's Tea Cups

BRIT TIP ✔

Fantasyland is definitely the place to bring your family if you are looking to meet a character or two, with more meet 'n' greet opportunities than any other zone in Disneyland Park. Check the daily programme for times and locations but don't expect to meet or interact with the characters outside of those times. Even if you do spot them walking through the park the most you'll get is a cheery wave.

Le Carrousel de Lancelot, though, it loads a large number of riders at one time so the queue is often not as long as it first appears.

Le Pays des Contes de Fées 34

- *7-minute guided outdoor boat ride*
- *Any age*
- *Average wait times under 20 minutes*

This outdoor boat ride leads guests through a maze of small islands on a 7-minute cruise of some of your favourite Disney scenes in miniature. The castle from *The Little Mermaid*, Rapunzel's tower, Mount Olympus and Hansel and Gretel's cottage can all be seen nestled amongst the rolling hills, showing some true Disney artistry in this hand-crafted village of buildings that all stand less than 2-metres tall. Be aware that this particular ride is frequently kept out of service during the winter months.

Casey Jr – le Petit Train du Cirque 33

- *2-minute gentle train-themed roller coaster*
- *Any age except for children under 1 year of age*
- *Average wait times 20 to 45 minutes*

For a bird's eye view of the Storybook Land seen in Le Pays des Contes de Fées boat ride, hop aboard the Casey Jr train for a gentle ride. Don't be fooled by the term 'roller coaster': this train ride is as soft as it gets and only really boasts a few twists and turns at moderate speed and a little gentle banking, making it perfectly safe for all ages.

it's a small world 36

- *10-minute indoor narrative boat ride*
- *Any age, especially under 8s*
- *Average wait times under 20 minutes*

This ride is a true Disneyland classic, having made its way over from the California and Orlando parks to become a popular and unmissable visual treat here in Europe too. The long queues quickly go down due to the high capacity of each motorised boat and the speed with which they load passengers. Take your seat and sit back as this classic ride takes you through a cavern divided into different sections dedicated to the various cultures and continents of the world, and populated by thousands of mechanical moving dolls. Extensively renovated for the 25th anniversary, the ride now

it's a small world

boasts new special effects, refurbished boats and state-of-the-art LED lighting. The soundtrack was also tinkered with to improve sound quality, but arguably the most noticeable audio update for riders is the inclusion of a voice yodelling along to the song in the Switzerland section.

Meet Mickey Mouse 29

- *2 to 3 minutes meet and greet*
- *Attraction photo with Photopass*
- *10:30 to 5pm everyday*
- *Any age*
- *Average wait time 60 to 90 minutes*

Always one for a bit of theatricality, Mickey Mouse can be found in his own special theatre, just next to the Disneyland Railroad Fantasyland Station. Join the queue as early as possible in the morning to go backstage and meet the famous magical Mouse himself, and don't forget to get a photo to remember this special moment!

Princess Pavilion 35

- *2 to 3 minutes meet and greet*
- *Attraction photo with Photopass*
- *Reservations from 10:15am everyday*
- *Any age*
- *Average wait time up to 90 minutes*

On the other side of **Alice's Curious Labyrinth** towers the pink façade of the **Princess Pavilion**: the perfect place to meet real Disney royalty. Again, if this is top of your to-do list during your Disneyland Paris trip, make sure you get here first thing. Reservations are made from 10:15am every day at the Pavilion itself. Check at City Hall as you enter the front gates of the park to find out which princesses are available for a meeting on that particular day if that's important to you.

Royal Castle Stage 37

- *Open-air seated show venue*
- *Mickey presents: Happy Anniversary Disneyland Paris*
- *The Starlit Princess Waltz*

A fixed venue for a variety of Disney spectaculars, this year continuing to feature 25th Anniversary specials (see page 101).

(see page 101)

BRIT TIP

Beginning on the hour and then at every subsequent 15 minutes, the outdoor clock at the top of **it's a small world** opens up to reveal a little clockwork parade of mechanical dolls set to – what else? – the its a small world song. A lovely little set piece, and easy to catch as it is so frequent.

BRIT TIP

Children who either dress up as a Disney character or bring a toy or doll of a Disney character with them always receive some special attention from the characters as it provides a talking point during their meeting.

Cinderella's carriage outside Auberge de Cendrillon.

Dining

Auberge de Cendrillon

- ■ €€€ - *Highly priced*
- ■ *Table Service*
- ■ *TripAdvisor rating: 3.5*

At the Auberge de Cendrillon (see also page 61) you can find traditional French cuisine in a royal fairy-tale setting, with the added opportunity to meet Cinderella herself, and her mice Suzy and Perla. Multiple characters such as Snow White, Sleeping Beauty and Prince Philip all frequent this eatery, performing two set-piece dances and spending time at each table talking to the seated guests. This character dining experience comes at a price of around €70 per adult and €40 per child, making it more suited to a one-off special event rather than a place you revisit time and time again. However, reviews rave about the 'helpful and friendly' staff, the effort made by the characters to talk to every child, and the well-presented 3-course menu on offer along with a welcome mocktail for grown-ups and a small parting gift for every child. Book a table in advance either through the Dining Reservation Service on +33 1 60 30 40 50 or at the Reception Desk of your Disney Hotel.

Au Chalet de la Marionette

- ■ € - *Low priced*
- ■ *Quick counter service*
- ■ *TripAdvisor rating: 3.5*

Just around the corner from the Auberge de Cendrillon lies this easy, quick lunchtime option. Contrary to the expectations conjured up by the name, this eatery provides a cross between American and Bavarian cuisine, offering various types of burgers and hot dogs. Some disinterested previous guests have noted that this is simply a 'burger joint that is dressed up poorly as something more interesting' whilst others have been much more complimentary of the quick service and ample tasty options available. The three set menus on offer range from around €12 to €15, and there is a children's menu for about €9 and various a la carte options.

Toad Hall Restaurant

- ■ € - *Low priced*
- ■ *Quick Counter Service*
- ■ *TripAdvisor rating: 3*

Toad Hall Restaurant adds a small breath of fresh air to an American cuisine-dominated eating experience, even if only with a plate of British fish and chips. Many guests have been a little put off by the high prices, whilst others have been happy with the large portions and the additional salad options on offer. There are three set menus ranging from around €12 to €15, a children's menu for about €9 and various a la carte options.

Fantasia Gelati

- ■ *€ - Low priced*
- ■ *Quick Counter Service*
- ■ *TripAdvisor rating: 4*

In the height of summer this small ice cream parlour is a very popular destination at any time of the day, sadly leading to a long queue. However, you can pick up large scoops of a delicious flavour of your choice for less than €4, making this small snack one of the cheapest throughout Disneyland Paris.

Pizzeria Bella Notte

- ■ *€ - Low priced*
- ■ *Quick Counter Service*
- ■ *TripAdvisor rating: 3*

This quick service pizzeria, themed as the restaurant from *Lady and the Tramp*, has both 'friendly staff' and an alternative type of cuisine on its side, even if the décor is a little dated. For less than €15, you can get a main meal, dessert and a drink, where the main is usually pasta or a pizza of your choice. Reviews have suggested that food is pretty basic, though.

Discoveryland

From the pushing forward of the American West over in Frontierland, Discoveryland takes the next great future frontier – space – as its central theme. Wander over into this metallic and neon world of rockets, scientific inventions and the mysteries of the universe to check out some of the park's most exciting attractions.

Putting Discoveryland at the forefront of the 25th Anniversary celebrations, 2017 saw the rebranding of the extremely popular Space Mountain: Mission 2 as the **Star Wars Hyperspace Mountain** and the launch of the brand new ride: **Star Tours: The Adventure Continues** on the same site as the old Star Tours ride.

These changes alongside the classic favourite attractions **Buzz Lightyear Laser Blast** and **Orbitron** continue to make Discoveryland one of the most popular – and busy! – lands in the park.

Toad Hall Restaurant.

BRIT TIP ✓

Pizzeria Bella Notte is often one of the quieter counter-service options during the peak hours for lunch and dinner as it lies a little off the beaten track.

BRIT TIP

If your child is desperate to take part in the **Jedi Training Academy**, report to **Videopolis** as soon as the park opens to try and be first in line: kids are selected on a 'first come, first served' basis.

Buzz Lightyear Laser Blast

- *5-minutes interactive dark cart ride*
- *Fastpass*
- *On-ride photo*
- *Age 5+*
- *Average wait times 45 to 75 minutes*

As you move through the dark gallery in your 'omnimover' cart, you are a Junior Space Ranger given the task of fighting evil Emperor Zurg's robot army. Fixed on the front of your space cruiser is a laser cannon for you and your companion to use against the moving targets. Every time you hit a target successfully you are rewarded with a certain number of points, which are then added up at the end to form your Star Command Ranking. Surprisingly addictive, this is one ride that families return to again and again as they strive to beat their score – and this means there is always a queue. Try visiting late in the evening when people are staking out their spot for Disney Illuminations for a relatively quiet time. An on-ride photo with your score printed on it is available if you would like a memento of your days as an intergalactic hero!

BRIT TIP

If you are planning to go on Buzz Lightyear multiple times to beat your earlier score and would like an on-ride photo, write down your photo number and score each time. You can then use the photo number to buy the photo with your winning high-score on it.

Orbitron

- *1-minute 30 seconds aerial carousel*
- *Age 5+*
- *Not suitable for pregnant women, or those with heart, back or neck problems*
- *Average wait times 30 to 60 minutes*

Apart from switching the elephant carriages for spaceships, this ride uses the same aerial carousel concept as **Dumbo the Flying Elephant** over in Fantasyland, although this time guests ride one behind the other as they shoot off into space in rockets of various colours, using their joy-sticks to adjust

BRIT TIP

Orbitron is an excellent ride to try at the end of the day when the park gets dark, as its bright neon lights give riders an even greater sense of being in a spaceship.

the height to suit them. For some reason, perhaps to do with the way the spaceships tilt during the ride, many people comment that it feels higher and much more thrilling than Dumbo, especially at the top. The feeling that you might fall out (which you definitely won't!) adds to the exhilaration. If your family are the right age to enjoy a more exciting version of Dumbo, don't just assume from the ground it will be the same as that but give it a try.

Autopia 40

- *5-minutes on-track driving circuit*
- *Minimum height: 0.81m; riders between 0.81m and 1.32m must be accompanied by someone over 1.32m.*
- *Age 8+*
- *Not suitable for pregnant women, or those with heart, back or neck problems*
- *Average wait times 60 to 90 minutes*

Orbitron

Take the wheel in your own colourful futuristic car as you race around this tree-lined track. You're in control in this small independent vehicle with its own working accelerator pedal, but don't worry – front and back bumpers and a guide rail keep you on track, and there are plenty of Disney pit stop workers on hand to help out if necessary. Some people find the cars quite heavy to drive and steer, and they usually require full acceleration to maintain a good speed. Riders may also be disconcerted by the fact that you won't necessarily follow the same route as the car that leaves immediately in front of you but may well be set on a different track. Remember this as you set off and you should avoid any minor panic that you've gone the wrong way! Note the rider requirements – and after that it should be fun all the way! Expect a long wait though, this is a slow loader.

Autopia

Star Wars Hyperspace Mountain 42

Previously Space Mountain: Mission 2

- *2 minutes 18 seconds big thrill indoor roller coaster*
- *5 star*
- *Fastpass*
- *Single Rider Service*
- *Minimum height: 1.32m*
- *Age 8+*
- *Not suitable for under 8s, pregnant women, or those with heart, back or neck problems*
- *Average wait times 60 to 90 minutes*

Star Wars Hyperspace Mountain.

BRIT TIP ✓

If the weather takes a turn for the worse, both **Buzz Lightyear** and **Star Wars Hyperspace Mountain** have indoor waiting areas to keep you dry and warm.

Launched and hyped up for the 2017 Anniversary celebrations as a new Star Wars attraction, this is essentially the same ride as the old Space Mountain: Mission 2 but given a new Star Wars theme and overlay to tie in with the launch of the new Star Tours on the other side of Discoveryland. The roller coaster itself is an unmissable high-thrills attraction. The carriage is cranked up to the launch pad as you hear an unnerving countdown just before you are propelled into space. If you have the composure to take a peek at the top, there is a cleverly placed window allowing you to look out over the parks. Then plunge into the depths of space to feel the full force of intergalactic travel. With three inversions, bright lights and a lot of turbulence, this is not an attraction for the faint-hearted.

Les Mystères du Nautilus 41
- ■ *Between 5 to 10 minutes Indoor walkthrough*
- ■ *Any age*
- ■ *Average wait times up to 5 minutes on very busy days*

Step down into Jules Verne's submerged Nautilus submarine for a brief encounter with the mysteries that lie at the bottom of the sea. With next to no queues throughout the year, this fun underground walkway provides a welcome break from either the glaring sun or the dampening rain, and is great for imaginative kids who don't mind seeing an octopus or two.

Arcade Beta 44
- ■ *Gaming arcade*
- ■ *Surcharge required*

This gaming arcade provides an indoor area for any families wanting to escape from the attractions and crowds for a while, especially as it is far from the path of the daily Parade. However, using the arcade machines comes at a surcharge, so don't forget to bring some extra Euros in your pocket or purse.

Star Tours

Star Tours: The Adventure Continues 45
- ■ *5-minute big thrill motion simulator*
- ■ *4 star*
- ■ *Fast Pass*
- ■ *Minimum height: 1.02m*
- ■ *Age 8+*
- ■ *Not suitable for under 3s, pregnant women, those with motion sickness, or those with heart, back or neck problems*
- ■ *Average wait times 15 to 45 minutes*

MEET THE CHARACTERS AT DISNEYLAND PARK

 Go to pages 59–61 for information on where to meet the characters at Disneyland Park or scan the QR code to open the Park Programme.

Opened in March 2017, this is a motion simulator ride in the same style as the previous **Star Tours** ride that it replaced. In a fun-filled 4-and-a-half minute whizz through the galaxy, riders enjoy scenes, locations and characters from all the *Star Wars* films from *Episode 1* to *Episode 7*. The visual special effects and motion make this a very realistic and thrilling ride that nevertheless remains suitable for almost all the family although be aware that a lot of the dialogue is in French only. In a change from the usual standard ride experience, each individual Star Tours ride takes a random selection of Star Wars movie segments as its backdrop, and with over 70 possible segment combinations available, this means that almost every ride is unique – a great bonus for repeat riders.

L'Astroport Services Interstellaires

- ■ *Gaming arcades*
- ■ *Surcharge required*

As visitors exit the Star Tours attraction, they are once again able to stop for a moment and play a couple of the arcade games available – for a surcharge. Find dance machines, racing games, and various space-themed options for both kids and grown-ups alike.

Dining

Café Hyperion

- ■ *€ - Low price*
- ■ *Quick counter service*
- ■ *TripAdvisor rating: 3*

American-style fast food is here given a futuristic space theme to satisfy even the pickiest of eaters. Burgers, chicken nuggets and salads are all available in set menus including desserts and drinks for less than €15 per person. There are Star Wars-themed options with green Yoda cupcakes and black Darth Vader burgers, adding a fun twist to a fast-food meal.

Buzz Lightyear's Pizza Planet Restaurant

- € - Low price
- Buffet service
- TripAdvisor rating: 3

At the Pizza Planet Restaurant, adults can eat for around €18 per head whilst kids can have as much pizza and pasta as they like for around €15. Previous guests have noted the slightly rundown features of this eatery, but thankfully this should all have been fully taken care of in the recent full refurbishments conducted in the last year.

Fireworks over Sleeping Beauty Castle

Visual attractions

The Forest of Enchantment: A Disney musical adventure...

- Chaparral Theatre, Frontierland
- Variously from spring 2017
- 20-minute show
- Any age
- Check park guide for times
- This show is in English

Held inside the **Chaparral Theatre** in Frontierland, which you can find next to the Disneyland Railroad Frontierland Depot, this show transports you to the heart of the jungle! Characters such as Tarzan, Pocahontas, Merida and Rapunzel – as well as King Louis and Baloo the bear – take you on a song-and-dance-filled adventure through an enchanted forest.

Frozen Sing-along

- *Chaparral Theatre, Frontierland*
- *Winter/Christmas 2017–18 season*
- *Any age*
- *Check park guide for times*

During the Christmas season, the **Chaparral Theatre** in Frontierland has Elsa, Anna and Olaf live on stage for a fun-filled sing-along of all the favourite songs from Frozen.

Mickey presents: Happy Anniversary Disneyland Paris

- *Royal Castle Stage, Fantasyland*
- *From 26 March 2017*
- *15-minute show*
- *Any age*
- *Every day at 12:20pm; 1:20pm; 2:20pm*

Held on the **Royal Castle Stage**, this is a brand-new, sparkling song-and-dance show to celebrate the 25th Anniversary. A host of all the favourite characters – including Woody, Jessie and Buzz, Alice in Wonderland, Pooh and the gang and, of course, the ubiquitous Mice – thrill and entertain in equal measure as fountain shoots out water in time to the music. The 15-minute running time makes this twice the length of some of the outdoor shows of the past and a real treat for Disney fans.

The Starlit Princess Waltz

- *Royal Castle Stage, Fantasyland*
- *From 26 March 2017*
- *20-minute show*
- *Any age*
- *Every day at 1:50pm; 4:30pm; 5:05pm; 6:15pm; 7:00pm*

The Starlit Princess Waltz.

BRIT TIP ☑

You can expect a bit of pushing and shoving as the parade draws near and late-comers try to squeeze in. Be prepared to make space for little children, especially at the front, but stand your ground if their parents try to join them! You will notice that the British etiquette towards pushing in doesn't really apply here but if you remain firm but polite you should find that late-comers just move on.

BRIT TIP ☑

If you have a pushchair, position yourself in the second row and stand directly behind it. The space it creates between you and the crowd should give you a great view.

All the favourite Disney Princesses perform on the **Royal Castle Stage** in an especially sparkly waltz against an evening backdrop of the Sleeping Beauty Castle and fountain. It's actually quite rare to see so many Disney Princesses perform together at the same time, making this an extra special opportunity introduced in the Anniversary year.

Jedi Training Academy

- *Videopolis Theatre, Discoveryland*
- *15-minute interactive show*
- *Variously from spring 2017*
- *Every day during high season at the following times: 1pm, 2pm, 3pm, 5:20pm, 6:15pm, 7:15pm*
- *Any age to watch; 7–12s to participate*

This interactive show, running at peak times only, selects a small group of young aspiring Jedis, between the ages of 7 and 12, to take part in a fun-filled training experience. Kids who want to take part need to sign up early at the **Videopolis** theatre. They will then be told to turn up 45 minutes before the start of their allotted show so that they can begin their Jedi training. Remember the places are given on a first come first served basis, so arrive early in the day to sign up! Reservations for places in the show start at 10:45am.

Disney Stars On Parade

- *40-minute show*
- *5:30pm everyday*
- *Any age*

Don't worry if you haven't found the time to meet a Disney character in person: you can see them all in action in the daily **Disney Stars On Parade** show. Fully updated for the 25th Anniversary this is a grand marching, dancing, musical parade with brand new floats, carriages, bright costumes and all the instantly recognisable princesses and characters – with the addition of a fire-breathing dragon! This new parade contains some elements not seen in the parades before, including computerised effects (*Finding Nemo* float) and live stunts (*Toy Story* float).

The parade makes its way from the 'it's a small world' attraction in Fantasyland, past the Pizzeria Bella Notte, around the outer edge of Discoveryland, around the Central Plaza and down Main Street USA to the Town Square. There are a few main viewing spots to stake out to ensure you have a perfect view of the action, but unfortunately you will have to arrive at these points up to an hour before the parade begins to beat the crowds. These viewing spots are:

- Next to 'it's a small world' to catch the beginning of the parade
- At the Royal Castle Stage – stand on the edge of Discoveryland
- Central Plaza
- Along Main Street – although this area is always crowded
- From the band stand in Town Square

Make sure you check on the day of your visit to ensure the parade is running, as sometimes it can be cancelled if it clashes with other events. The parade will also be cancelled if the weather is wet or disruptive. Check at the information desk in City Hall if you need more information on the day, or scan the QR code to visit the Disneyland Paris website

 Scan the QR code above for more information about the parades in the park.

Disney Illuminations
- *20-minute show (approximately)*
- *Any age*
- *Whenever the park closes (check seasonal park closure times)*

The award-winning and hugely popular Disney Dreams! show was replaced in 2017 with Disney Illuminations, specially created for the 25th Anniversary. Set in front of the magical Sleeping Beauty Castle, it takes place every night at park closing time (weather permitting) and takes the spectacular combination of fireworks, lasers, water fountains, projections, colour and music of Disney Dreams! and uses them in a new display featuring scenes from the classic films. *The Lion King*, *The Little Mermaid*, *Frozen* and – what else? – *Star Wars* are among those you will see in this impressive show, although note that much of the dialogue and several of the favourite songs are in French. Other extra firework displays take place on select nights throughout the year such as Bastille Day and New Year's Day and are then followed by Disney Illuminations.

BRIT TIP ☑

The fire effects used in these night-time displays are surprisingly hot as well as dazzling if you stand close to the castle. If you stand further back along Main Street you may find that you can actually enjoy the show better. The projections on to the castle are high enough to be seen by everyone.

Disney Illuminations

Guests gather in Central Plaza to view the show and it's worth staking out a place at least an hour beforehand. The best position to enjoy the full effects of the show is towards the entrance point of Central Plaza from Main Street; further forward is too close.

Mickey's Goodnight Kiss

- *Disney Railroad, Main Street Station*
- *Whenever the park closes (check seasonal park closure times)*

Not strictly an attraction as such, but a lovely little touch from the early days of Disneyland Paris reintroduced for the 25th Anniversary. Mickey Mouse stands on the balcony of Main Street Station to wave goodbye to the guests as they depart after the end of Disney Illuminations.

Princesses and Pirates Festival

- *31 March to 31 May*

This brand-new festival provides something for everyone themed around sparkling princesses and adventurous pirates.

Disney FanDaze Inaugural Party

- *First weekend in June*

Disney is launching a new series of events, specifically designed to celebrate Disney fans the world over. During the first weekend in June, Disneyland Paris will host its FanDaze Inaugural Party featuring more than fifty Disney characters (some rarely seen before), the *Max Live!* concert, *Dance Your*

Ducktales parade, special menus and exclusive souvenirs. In addition, fans will be able to dress as their favourite Disney character and enjoy an evening of attractions exclusively for them at Walt Disney Studios Park.

Marvel Super Heroes
■ *10 June to September 30*

The summer season at Disneyland Paris sees the arrival of the Marvel Super Heroes including Spider-Man, Captain America, Star-Lord, Iron Man, Thor and Black Widow. Look out for meet and greets with the characters, stunning shows and almost certainly an epic extravaganza to close the 25th Anniversary celebrations.

Tours

Disneyland Park Tour

Take a 2-hour guided walking tour of Disneyland Park and learn all the secrets behind the workings and the history of the five lands. This fascinating tour gives you a special insight into the choices made by Walt Disney himself when he first came up with the idea of a Disney theme park and how he brought the fairy tales off the page and into real life. Departure is from City Hall at 1pm and 2pm and costs €25 per adult and €15 per child (3–11).

Reserve your place on the tour before you arrive by emailing the Disney Special Activities Team at **dlp.disney.special. activities@disney.com**.

VIP Tours

You can also create your own personalised tour with the VIP option. A tour guide accompanies you throughout the park for a certain amount of time, and gives you all the inside Disney knowledge as you go. They can even help you choose which rides and attractions to go on next, or which shows you should see throughout the day as well as helping you to book reservations for restaurants and shows.

With the VIP tour option, you also get an extra special spot to see the Disney Magic on Parade go by, as well as a perfect viewpoint from which to watch the Disney Dreams! night-time show.

Book in advance by emailing the Disney Special Activities Team at **dlp.disney.special.activities@disney.com**.

PARK DETAILS

OPENING HOURS	**Low Season (Autumn and Winter)** ■ Monday to Thursday: 10 – 7pm ■ Friday and Saturday: 9pm ■ Sunday: 8pm **High Season (Spring and Summer)** ■ Monday to Sunday: 10am – 10pm (11pm in school holidays) Times subject to change without notice – keep up to date through the website **www.disneylandparis.co.uk**
PARKING	Parking for Disney Hotel guests is free at both your hotel and in the Disney Car Park in front of the parks. For non-Disney Hotel visitors, parking in the Disney Car Park costs the following: ■ Cars €20 per day ■ Vehicles over 2 metres high €20 per day ■ Campervans €35 per day ■ Motorbikes €15 per day

Scan the QR code for park opening times.

ATTRACTIONS	At-a-glance age group suitability (height restrictions have been taken into account)			
	Under 5s	**5–8s**	**9–12s**	**Over 12s**
Main Street Vehicles	•	•	•	•
Disneyland Railroad	•	•	•	•
Thunder Mesa Riverboats	•	•	•	•
La Cabane des Robinson	•	•	•	•
'it's a small world'	•	•	•	•
Alice's Curious Labyrinth	•	•	•	•
Disney Stars on Parade	•	•	•	•
Le Passage Enchanté d'Aladdin	•	•	•	•
Pirates of the Caribbean	•	•	•	•
Disney Illuminations	•	•	•	•
Peter Pan's Flight	•	•	•	•
La Plage des Pirates play area	•	•	•	
Les Voyages de Pinocchio	•	•	•	
Le Carrousel de Lancelot	•	•	•	
Blanche Neige et les Sept Nains	•	•	•	

ATTRACTIONS	At-a-glance age group suitability (height restrictions have been taken into account)			
	Under 5s	5–8s	9–12s	Over 12s
Pocahontas Indian Village	•	•	•	
Le Pays des Contes de Fées	•	•	•	
Casey Jr	•	•	•	
Meet Mickey	•	•	•	
Adventure Isle	•	•	•	
Princesses Pavilion	•	•	•	
Mad Hatter's Tea Cups	•	•	•	
Orbitron	•	•	•	
Dumbo the Flying Elephant	•	•		
Buzz Lightyear's Laser Blast		•	•	•
La Tanière du Dragon		•	•	•
Les Mystères du Nautilus		•	•	•
Autopia		•	•	•
Rustler Roundup Shootin' Gallery		•	•	•
Phantom Manor		•	•	•
L'Astroport Services Interstellaires		•	•	•
Big Thunder Mountain		•	•	•
Star Tours: The Adventure Continues			•	•
Star Wars Hyperspace Mountain			•	•
Indiana Jones and the Temple of Peril			•	•

Fantasyland.

7 Walt Disney Studios

Walt Disney Studios offers a change of pace and a different atmosphere from the Disneyland Park. As the name suggests, entering the Studios draws you not only into the magical world of your favourite Disney TV programmes and movies, but beyond the camera lens to witness all the behind-the-scenes action.

Entrance to Walt Disney Studios

Walt Disney Studios offers a change of pace and a different atmosphere from the Disneyland Park. As the name suggests, entering the Studios draws you not only into the magical world of your favourite Disney TV programmes and movies, but beyond the camera lens to witness all the behind-the-scenes action.

Find yourself centre stage on larger-than-life film sets amidst the dazzling lights, or take your place in the director's chair to witness the stunts, special effects and dazzling artistry that makes Disney appealing to all age groups.

At half the size of the neighbouring park, Walt Disney Studios is divided into four manageable sections – the Front Lot, Toon Studio, the Backlot and the Production Courtyard – all taking their own unique twist on the central theme of Hollywood movie-making and Tinsel Town glamour.

There is a big emphasis on extravagant spectacles and shows, of which there are plenty to try, which range from live character performances for tiny tots to stunt car displays for the older audiences. The Studios provide the perfect opportunity for your family to see some of their favourite stars on stage in the likes of **Stitch Live!** and **Disney Junior Live on Stage!** or even in person. Mickey, Buzz Lightyear, Spiderman and a whole variety of Disney characters can be found in either Toon Studio or Backlot ready to meet their fans!

In this park, the big-draw attractions certainly don't scrimp on thrill-factor. When compared with the Disneyland Park, there are far more high-speed rides for teenagers and adults here. These include the **Twilight Zone Tower of Terror, Crush's Coaster**, the **Rock 'n' Roller Coaster starring Aerosmith**, and

PARK TACTICS

Try to plan out your day so that you get a good mix of shows and rides, as well as some well-timed food and drink stops. The Studios can seem a bit show-heavy at times and some of these shows cater to the younger ages, which may not suit every member of your family. Try to decide which you want to see and check the show times on one of the programmes at the front gates as soon as you arrive. Once you have organised your schedule for the day, do the rides of your choice in between the show times. Remember, you can leave and re-enter either the Studios or the Disneyland Park whenever you like on the day of your visit – just keep your ticket to hand and have your hand stamped if you want to re-enter the same park later the same day.

If you aren't too keen on the shows and are going to give these a miss, the rest of the Studios can be easily explored in two to three hours in quieter times of the year and certainly in one day even in peak time.

Certain rides in the Studios are known for their long queues (around two hours at their peak in summer). These include **Crush's Coaster, Ratatouille: The Adventure, RC Racer** and **Toy Soldiers Parachute Drop**. Try either to hit these early in the morning or keep an eye on the wait times throughout the day to take advantage of a quiet spells. Of course you can invest in a FastPass (see page 50) if available.

If you have a mix of ages, likes and dislikes in your party consider splitting up for part of the day to focus on – and queue for – your personal choice of shows and rides.

There is a Single Rider Service on many popular rides – such as Ratatouille: The Adventure and Crush's Coaster – which can help you cut the queues if you aren't worried about being separated from a companion. However, always make sure you check the times on the boards carefully before you join any Single Rider queue – at peak times it can be almost as long as the regular queue.

As most of the attractions are either sheltered or indoors, the Studios are perfect for a rainy day outing, or as a place to retreat to if the weather suddenly turns sour.

the **RC Racer**, which are all extremely popular. One of the newest additions – **Ratatouille: The Adventure** – has also proved a hit for audiences of all ages, even without the promise of loop-the-loops or high G-forces.

The majority of the attractions in this park are indoors, happily removing them from the elements during the colder months while providing some welcome shelter from the heat during summer – summer in Paris can be very hot and humid.

Compared to the Disneyland Park, you'll find the dining opportunities in the Studios to be a little thin on the ground, but all the same, whether you are looking for a fast-food fix at the **Restaurant en Coulisse** or a sit-down extravaganza à

Walt Disney Studios
A list rides | **B list** rides

Front Lot

1   Walt Disney Studios store
2   Studio Photo
3   Disney Studio 1
4   Les Légendes d'Hollywood
5   Restaurant en Coulisse

Production Courtyard

6   Place des Stars
7   Disney Junior – Live on Stage!
8   **Stitch Live!**
9   Restaurant des Stars
10   **The Twilight Zone™ Tower of Terror**
11   Studio Tram Tour

The Backlot

12   **Armageddon: les Effets Speciaux**
13   Disney Blockbuster Café
14   Rock around the Shop
15   **Rock 'n' Roller Coaster starring Aerosmith**
16   **Moteurs...Action! Stunt Show Spectacular**
17   Café des Cascadeurs
18   **Ratatouille: The Adventure**
19   Bistrot Chez Rémy

Toy Story Playland

20   RC Racer
21   Slinky Dog Zigzag Spin
22   Toy Soldiers Parachute Drop

Toon Studio

23   Cars Quatre Roues Rallye
24   **Crush's Coaster**
25   Les Tapis Volants – Flying Carpets over Agrabah
26   **Animagique**
27   Disney Animation Gallery
28   **Art of Disney Animation**

Scan the QR code above for an online map of Walt Disney Studios.

BRIT TIP ☑

If you arrive before the Studios open at 10am, you will usually be allowed to enter the park shopping area early. This means you will get to see the set 'wake up' with its magical light and sound sequence and its call to 'Action'!

la Française at the relatively new option **Bistrot Chez Rémy**, there is something to suit every palate and pocket.

Situated between the Disney Village and the Disneyland Park, you will find the Studios opposite the easy-access car park and Marne-la-Vallee/Chessy station.

Front Lot

Walk through the front gates of Walt Disney Studios and you immediately find yourself in the Front Lot and the world of cinematic creation. This area expertly creates a Disney movie-magic atmosphere by transforming the world around you into a Hollywood film set with bright lights, colour and fun characters that Disney is known for.

Place des Frères Lumière

Guests enter through the Place des Frères Lumière, named after the Lumière brothers (Auguste Marie Louis Nicolas and Louis Jean) who are considered to be the first ever filmmakers in history. The square's central fountain shows an iconic scene from Disney's Fantasia, with a stone Mickey Mouse mischievously commanding a selection of mops and buckets under the power of his wizard's hat and creating spouts of tumbling water.

To the left as you enter is the meet-and-greet venue for Goofy or his Disney pals. Meander straight across the square to the other side of the fountain and you find yourself at the Walt Disney Studios Store: a general outlet supplying plush toys and Disney memorabilia. On the right side of the square, just past the studio services you will find the Stroller and Wheelchair rental station.

Disney Studio 1

Disney Studio 1 **3**

Looking up at the colossal size of Studio 1, it is not surprising to discover that this is one of the biggest buildings not only in the Studios, but also across the entirety of Disneyland Paris. This cavernous indoor space is created to represent Hollywood at the height of its golden era, with a boulevard stretching down its centre, and glamorous store fronts and lavish set designs from the 1920s and 1960s along either side. You are the star on this film set and have the surrounding props and neon light to prove it, as well as glimpses of many of the iconic characters and backdrops many people will recognise.

Dining

Restaurant en Coulisse
- *Quick counter service*
- *€ - low price*
- *TripAdvisor rating: 3*

On your right as you enter Studio 1 is Restaurant en Coulisse, offering American-style burgers, fast food and various other options in keeping with the Hollywood theme. TripAdvisor reviews vary from heralding their produce as the 'best burgers in Disneyland' to comments on its not too hasty service. However, for less than €15 per person, Restaurant en Coulisse is a quick option for any time of the day. This eatery always draws crowds by simply being set inside the impressive backdrop of Studio 1.

Toon Studio

Leaving Studio 1, guests will find themselves in another square with a Mickey Mouse centrepiece: this time there is a sculpture showing the iconic mouse holding the hand of his creator, Walt Disney. Turn right and you enter Toon Studio where the cartoons come to life before your very eyes!

Toon Studio

Art of Disney Animation
- *20-minute guided tour + optional drawing time*
- *Any age*
- *Average wait times less than 30 minutes*

Where better to begin your journey into the origins of Disney creation than by walking through the history of animation? After an initial wait in an area where you can read about the history of animation and examine some objects used in early cartoons, this indoor attraction begins with a film of Walt Disney himself paying tribute to early animators, then a cinema showing of classic clips and excerpts from Disney movies. Expect to laugh and cry at the funny and touching moments from the much-loved films we all remember. This is followed by a live show in which the art of cartoon animation is demonstrated. The cinema clips are silent, set to music, but the live show is in French with an English translation provided through headphones. At the end of the show, visit the various Animation Stations to try your hand at creating your own Disney characters.

BRIT TIP ☑

If you don't like the look of the **Art of Disney Animation** show, it's still worth checking out the Animation Stations. Enter through the exit doors straight into the Animation Stations area while a show is taking place and it should be relatively quiet and easy to find a spot at one of the seated Stations for a spot of creative drawing.

Animagique Theatre

Animagique Theatre 26

- *Mickey and the Magician*
- *20-minute show*
- *At scheduled times*
- *Any age, especially under 8s*

Formerly the home of the Animagique live puppet show, this theatre is hosting a new show – Mickey and the Magician – from March 2017 until January 2018. Mickey is given the task of cleaning up the great Magician's studio but he can't resist trying a little magic himself. He is accidentally transported to the most magical worlds where he meets the Genie from Aladdin, the Fairy Godmother, Lumière, Rafiki and Elsa who conjure up some amazing illusions. With singing and dancing from Aladdin, The Lion King, Frozen and more, and illusions by the acclaimed magician Paul Kieve, it's sure to be a big hit for all the family.

Riding the Flying Carpets Over Agrabah

Flying Carpets Over Agrabah 25

- *1 minute 30 seconds aerial carousel*
- *Fastpass*
- *Any age; especially 5–12s*
- *Not suitable for pregnant women*
- *Average wait times under 20 minutes*

A surprising addition to the Toon Studio, **Flying Carpets Over Agrabah** sits in the corner of the lot right next to the Animagique theatre. This aerial carousel adds a welcome outdoor ride to a so-far show-packed park. It is rumoured that this *Aladdin*-themed ride – where guests sit on the back of flying carpets which gently float through the air around the Genie's golden lamp – was originally intended for the Agrabah area of Adventureland over in the Disneyland Park, but was redistributed at the last minute. This turned out to be an excellent change of plan, as this now means the Studios have a ride similar to Disneyland Park's **Dumbo** attraction, but often with a less intimidating queue – and a Fastpass option as well.

Crush's Coaster 24

- *2 minutes 20 seconds big thrill spinning roller coaster*
- *Single Rider Service*
- *Minimum height: 1.07m*
- *Age: 8+*
- *Not suitable for under 8s, pregnant women, or those with heart, back or neck problems*
- *Average wait times 90 to 120 minutes*

It's not surprising that **Crush's Coaster** quickly became one of the most popular rides in Disneyland Paris when it opened in 2007, as it promises both high-thrills and a convincing Finding Nemo-themed backdrop. Guests are strapped into their turtle-shell cart and sent on a spinning coaster ride with twists and turns in the turbulent currents of the East Australian Current. Catch a glimpse of some of your favourite characters from the film in the ride's dark, glowing indoor setting, including Crush, Squirt, Nemo and Marlin as well as Bruce the shark skulking around his sunken submarine.

Crush's Coaster.

This ride's popularity does have its downsides, with long queues regardless of the season, and no FastPass. To try to make the wait less dull, Disney offers Crush's Coaster Game, which can be accessed online through the free Wi-Fi available. This gives you a bit of on-line entertainment as you help Crush catch starfish and dodge obstacles to become the surf champion of the EAC.

Cars Quatre Roues Rallye 23

- *1 minute 30 seconds alternative teacups ride*
- *Any age, especially under 12s*
- *Not suitable for pregnant women*
- *Average wait times 30 to 60 minutes*

Directly across from **Crush's Coaster**, jump aboard one of the colourful selection of motorcars and get ready to race around the track! This Disney Pixar Cars-themed ride is perfect for guests both big and small, spinning and twisting the vehicles on a turntable to give anyone who loves the **Mad Hatter's Tea Cups** a whole new, revamped experience of a theme-park classic.

BRIT TIP

The **Cars** ride is a very slow loader and doesn't have the biggest capacity so the queues are often extremely long and there is no Fastpass. Make a beeline for it as soon as you arrive if you have young children.

Ratatouille

As one of the newest additions to the Disneyland Paris repertoire, and boasting a little something for everyone, the Ratatouille area of Toon Studio is a must-see. Check out the gushing fountain with its carved rats holding up bubbling champagne bottles, and marvel at the detail of the Parisian architecture, bringing a chic dose of French culture to this small corner of the Studios.

BRIT TIP

For all your **Ratatouille**-themed souvenirs, as well as other plush toys, Disney collectibles and art works head to Chez Marianne.

Ratatouille: The Adventure `18`

- *5 minute cart ride with special effects*
- *Fastpass*
- *Single Rider Service*
- *All ages but may frighten little ones*
- *Average wait times 90 to 150 minutes*

Pick up your 3D glasses from the front desk and make your way to Gusteau's famous restaurant for this new twist on the classic narrative cart ride. **Ratatouille: The Adventure** is brought to you with all of the special effects and latest technology you could expect emerging fresh out of the creative studios. Step into the rat-shaped trackless ride vehicle and enter a world of towering scenery, oversized kitchen utensils and surrounding 3D screens depicting all of the culinary action from a rat's point of view: you may be as small as a rodent, but you are a big part of the action on this exciting 4D journey!

Ratatouille

Dining

Bistrot Chez Rémy

- €€€ - Highly priced
- Table service
- TripAdvisor rating: 4

Bistrot Chez Remy

Offering traditional French bistro cuisine, Chez Rémy combines cute over-sized 'rat's-eye view' décor – with champagne cork seats, cocktail umbrellas and giant plate dividers – with a fancy French dose of *je ne sais quoi*. Reviews on TripAdvisor are mainly positive, heralding the eatery as 'one of the best restaurants in Disney', providing 'lots of fun and something different'. A meal with a starter and main course places you at about €30, while the Émile Menu adds a dessert and a drink for just under €40.

As a central part of the Ratatouille story, this eatery is truly not to be missed – even if it means you simply poke your head through the door or peer through the windows to get a glimpse of the delightful, creative décor. Chez Rémy is pretty popular so make a reservation just to be on the safe side through the Dining Reservation Service on +33 1 60 30 40 50, or book at the reception desk of your Disney Hotel.

Toy Story Playland

Walk through the monkey-barrel tunnel and you will be shrunk down to the size of Mr Potato Head or even Woody himself in Toy Story Playland! The eye really is in the detail here where domino pieces and K'NEX form the fences lining the path, while giant Christmas lights crisscross overhead.

RC Racer 20

- 1 minute big thrill half-pipe roller coaster
- Single Rider Service
- Minimum height: 1.20m
- Age 8+
- Not suitable for pregnant women or those with heart, back or neck problems
- Average wait times 60 to 90 minutes

Big thrills meet thematic brilliance in the **RC Racer** half-pipe roller coaster, putting you in the driving seat of a giant toy car. Feel the speed as you reach heights of up to 24 metres as you zoom from one vertical extreme to another. At only a minute long this can seem like a disappointingly short ride after the extremely long wait times in high season, however, for others a minute will be quite long enough!

BRIT TIP

If you don't like the rocking Pirate Galleon type of rides common in UK theme parks, you almost certainly won't like **RC Racer**. It's the same type of motion but at about 5-times the speed!

Toy Story Playland

Slinky Dog Zigzag Spin

Toy Soldiers Parachute Drop

Slinky Dog Zigzag Spin 21

- ■ *1 minute 30 seconds circular chase ride*
- ■ *Any age*
- ■ *Not suitable for pregnant women*

If the **RC Racer** isn't for you, then the **Slinky Dog Zigzag Spin** is an appealing alternative just across the pathway. This circular chase ride has the popular plastic pooch chasing his tail around the track while you sit on his back for the ride, offering a tame but enjoyable experience for both children and adults alike.

Toy Soldiers Parachute Drop 22

- ■ *1 minute free-fall winch tower*
- ■ *Single Rider Service*
- ■ *Age 5+*
- ■ *Minimum height: 81cm*
- ■ *Average wait times 60 to 90 minutes*

The last stop as you leave Toy Story Playland is the towering **Toy Soldiers Parachute Drop**. As one of the most popular attractions in Disneyland Paris, the wait during summer might feel like a training exercise in itself, but it is certainly worth it for the enjoyable thrill and the view from the top. This free-fall winch tower pulls the buckled-in army trainees up into the sky before releasing the parachutes for an 82 foot drop, giving you a slight stomach-lurching thrill: what you might call the child-friendly alternative to the **Twilight Zone Tower of Terror**!

Production Courtyard

From one film set to another, the Production Courtyard takes you from the Pixar world of toys and tiny creatures to a miniature Hollywood Boulevard, complete with the iconic Hollywood sign. This zone also includes the Place des Stars, which features various shows and attractions, in particular the infamous **Twilight Zone Tower of Terror**.

Studio Tram Tour: Behind the Magic 11

- 15-minute tram tour
- Guests may get splashed
- Age 5+; explosions and loud noises may frighten little ones
- Average wait times 30 to 60 minutes

Having exited the Toon Studio from the Toy Story Playland, guests can immediately take a right and find themselves beneath the Hollywood sign and at the entrance to the Studio Tram Tour. The fan sites have been awash with rumours over recent years that this attraction was due to receive a full renovation and update with new scenery, or could even close altogether to make way for something new. However, its recent short closure during the EEP works simply gave it a bit of a tidy-up and some fresh paint and the ride itself is currently still the original version which opened along with the Studios Park in 2002. This guided experience, narrated by Jeremy Irons, takes you behind the scenes to witness the iconic props and explosive special effects used to make some of your favourite action scenes. Move from full-scale movie backdrops of city scenery to the Catastrophe Canyon film set to witness all of the destructive elements in action – warning: you might get a little wet in this 20-minute tour.

The Twilight Zone Tower of Terror 10

- 2 minute 25 seconds big thrill vertical drop ride
- Fastpass
- On-ride photos
- Minimum height: 1.02m
- Age 12+
- Not suitable for pregnant women, or those with heart, back or neck problems or high blood pressure
- Average wait times 60 to 90 minutes

Based on a real luxury Hollywood apartment building, and bringing all of the mystery of the TV series *The Twilight Zone* to life, the **Tower of Terror** is not a ride for the faint-hearted.

BRIT TIP

Sit toddlers and under-5s in the middle of your row of seats, not beside either window. This will protect them from most of the water and from the heat of the fire effects in **Catastrophe Canyon** and should help to make the ride less frightening for them.

Studio Tram Tour

The Twilight Zone Tower of Terror

Enter the dilapidated front lobby of the abandoned and haunted hotel before being ushered into the library for a 5-minute pre-ride introduction by The Twilight Zone creator, Rod Serling, who sets the ghostly scene.

The only way out is the possessed service elevator, which works as a vertical drop ride, promising a deathly plummet from great heights before switching to lurch you back up those 13 unlucky storeys once again. Don't miss the ghostly special effects as you are winched up to the top and the ghosts beckon you into the next world.

CinéMagique (closed)

One of the Studios Park's signature attractions, **CineMagique** closed permanently in March 2017. With recent confirmation from Disney that some new **Marvel** attractions are in pre-production for Walt Disney Studios, it looks very likely that this will be the venue for a brand-new Marvel superheroes stunt show.

Disney Junior Live on Stage! 7

- 25-minute live show
- Under 8s
- Shows at set times

Continue around the Place des Stars at the centre of the Production Courtyard and you will find yourself at the front doors of **Disney Junior Live on Stage!** When it was launched in 2009 as Playhouse Disney Live on Stage! this was a very appealing show for pre-schoolers as it featured live-action puppet versions of familiar TV shows. Now rebranded in line with the TV channel name change, unfortunately the TV shows referenced in the show are now rarely shown on UK television, making the participation element of the show not as good for British children as it once was. The small size of the puppets and the timeless appeal of Mickey, Minnie and the gang still make this show worth seeing though, especially for the under-5s.

There are around seven to eight performances per day, alternating between English and French; times vary from day to day. Check the daily Park Programme or the board at the venue on the day of your visit to confirm the show times.

Stitch Live! 8

- *15-minute live show*
- *Any age especially under 8*
- *Shows at set times*

If you aren't yet full to the brim of fabulous shows, then Stitch Live! promises something a little different to the average performance. Using amazing real-time computer animation technology, an on-screen furry, blue Stitch talks to, interacts with and sings along with the unsuspecting crowd, to the wonder of both children and adults alike. How do they do it? Come and witness this 15-minute show for yourself to try to figure out the magic behind bringing this loveable creature to life. Show times and available languages are sometimes published on the Disneyland website, but they vary from day to day. They are also listed outside the venue itself, so do some prior planning to factor this particular performance into your day.

Dining

Restaurant des Stars 9

- *€€ - Moderately priced*
- *Buffet style meal*
- *Reservations accepted*
- *TripAdvisor: 3.5*

Before you wander into the action-packed attractions waiting for you in the Backlot zone, this might be the perfect opportunity for you and your family to take a seat at the Restaurant des Stars. This eatery provides an all-you-can-eat buffet for around €30 per adult and €17 per child (3–11 years), offering a broad choice of international dishes, both hot and cold. The Art Deco décor and photos of famous film stars lining the walls set the scene. Reviews on TripAdvisor lean heavily towards positive comments, praising the 'good selection' and the 'friendly staff'. Restaurant des Stars offers an alternative sit-down meal choice to Chez Remy over in the Ratatouille area, with a greater variety and quantity of food within a more moderate price range. Highly popular, especially at peak times, it's worth making a prior reservation, through the Dining Reservation Service on +33 1 60 30 40.

BRIT TIP

You don't need to be a fan of the film *Lilo and Stitch*, or even have seen it, to enjoy **Stitch Live!**. It's a really funny, entertaining show for kids and adults alike.

BRIT TIP

Take bottles of water with you to fill up at the water fountains dotted around the park and a few croissants or sandwiches in your backpack to keep you going through the day.

Backlot

As one of the least identifiable zones in Disneyland Studios, the Backlot takes high thrills and movie action as its central theme. It has more to offer teenagers and adults than the other areas, with its focus on fast cars and the sci-fi action adventure Armageddon.

BRIT TIP

The special effects used in **Armageddon** and **Moteurs...Action! Stunt Show** are pretty intense so be absolutely sure they are suitable for your children before you take them in. Perhaps ask one parent or adult to test them out while the rest of the group enjoy a kids' show or ride.

Armageddon: les Effets Spéciaux

- *20 minutes indoor special effects tour and show*
- *Age 8 +; fire and explosions may frighten little ones*
- *Not suitable for pregnant women*
- *Average wait times less than 30 minutes*

Take your place at Armageddon: Les Effets Spéciaux as a member of the crew on the film set of a space station that is being hit by a meteorite shower. Be ready to see some serious pyrotechnics and special effects as the ceiling crumbles, pipes burst, and things start to explode around you. The whole experience lasts about 20 minutes, and occurs indoors.

BRIT TIP

Directly opposite the entrance to **Rock 'n' Roller Coaster**, don't miss **Les Parapluies de Cherbourg** (Umbrellas of Cherbourg). If you stand and pose for a picture underneath the umbrella fixed to the wall, at certain – random – times you might get an unexpected shower, *Singin' In The Rain* style! If you're passing and you notice the ground is wet in that area, you'll know the showers are in operation.

Rock 'n' Roller Coaster starring Aerosmith

- *1 minute 22 seconds big thrill indoor roller coaster*
- *Fastpass*
- *Age: 12 +*
- *Not suitable for under 8s, pregnant women, or those with heart, back or neck problems*
- *Minimum height: 1.2m*
- *Average wait times 20 to 45 minutes*

This indoor rollercoaster combines concert-style rock music from the band Aerosmith with the thrilling twists and turns of a roller coaster experience. Reaching up to 100kmph in less than 3 seconds and putting your body through about 4.5 Gs – clocking more G-force than your average astronaut – you will experience some 'Sweet Emotion' on this unique ride. State-of-the art technology provides each SoundTracker train with a unique Aerosmith soundtrack on board and a different array of accompanying lights every trip, providing a new experience each time you ride.

Moteurs... Action! Stunt Show Spectacular 16

- *40-minute car stunt show*
- *Age: 7+; may frighten younger guests*
- *Show at set times*

Our final stop is the Moteurs.... Action! live motor stunt show! These death-defying sequences, featuring Lightning McQueen himself from Disney Pixar's Cars, bring the magic of action-movie car chases to the arena in front of your very eyes, with the added excitement of some audience participation. Some of the visual effects such as a man on fire and the loud noises may frighten some children so it's worth trying this one yourself beforehand if you're unsure. The show lasts about 45 minutes and occurs around three times per day between 11:00am and 4:00pm; check your programme on the day to get the exact information you need.

Moteurs...Action! Stunt Show Spectacular

Dining

Café des Cascadeurs 17

- *€ - Low prices*
- *Table Service*
- *TripAdvisor: 3.5*

Take a seat in this authentic, metallic caravan-turned-diner for a real 1950s Americana experience on a budget. Main meals hit a maximum of €15, which usually include a premium burger with either fries or a side salad. This eatery has been generally rated as 'actually a nice place to eat', providing an 'excellent diner-style service', while other reviews have been less warm and complained about cold food.

Disney Blockbuster Café 13

- € - low prices
- Quick counter service
- TripAdvisor: 3

Opposite the Rock 'n' Roller Coaster you can easily find the large props warehouse that holds the Blockbuster Café. Sandwiches, pizzas and pasta dishes are on offer here for a potentially healthier selection than in most other Disney eateries, setting you back around €15 for a set menu, or around €7 for a sandwich. TripAdvisor reviews vary from praising this establishment as a 'lovely surprise' to putting it down as merely 'very mediocre'. However, being able to eat among the collection of Iron Man and Pirates of the Caribbean props is surely a selling point.

Visual attractions

Star Wars: A Galaxy Far Far away

- Place des Stars, Production Courtyard
- 13 January – 25 March 2018
- Any age
- Times vary; check daily programme

Right in the centre of the Production Courtyard is this large open space which has long been used for Disney visual spectaculars. In previous years, the Stars 'n' Cars parade would culminate here with characters dismounting from their vehicles to put on a song and dance display unlike anything in the Disneyland Park.

As part of the 25th Anniversary celebrations, the 'Season of the Force', which ran early in 2017 is making a come-back in 2018. Live Star Wars characters and special effects are used in the show to truly bring the cinematic feel of 'The Force' from the films to life.

First Order March

- Place des Stars, Production Courtyard
- 13 January – 25 March 2018
- Any age
- Times vary; check daily programme

In combination with the **Galaxy Far Far Away** display, Disney also offers this extra Star Wars-themed extravaganza. Captain Phasma leads the storm troopers in an impressive live show in which they harness their galactic power to dazzle and astound the watching crowd. The show may move to Discoveryland in the Disneyland Park for summer 2018.

Star Wars: A Galactic Celebration

- *Place des Stars, Production Courtyard*
- *13 January – 25 March 2018*
- *Any age*
- *Times vary; check daily programme*

Another spectacular visual feast for Star Wars fans, this time in the evening with film projections, special effects and appearances from classic Star Wars characters. Scenes from the new film *Star Wars: The Last Jedi* have been added in for 2018.

Tours

Walt Disney Studios Tour

To take the Walt Disney Studios Tour, contact the Special Activities team in advance to book at **dlp.disney.special. activities@disney.com**. Guests meet at 3pm (although the time may change due to parades and shows) at the Studio Services on the right as you enter the Place des Frères Lumière. The tour lasts one hour 30 minutes and costs €25 per adult; €15 per child (3 to 11); under-3s go free. It takes you through the history of cinema and looks at the influence Walt Disney had on the magical world of film. You will also experience a real working studio where modern animation and special effects are created on a daily basis.

The Tower of Terror Tour

If a trip to the Tower of Terror is not enough for you and you are looking to get some more behind-the-scenes action, book you and your family on to the Tower of Terror Tour.

This one-hour tour departs from Guest Relations at the entrance of Walt Disney Studios, beginning at 9.10am on Wednesdays and Saturdays. Follow your guide through the deserted Hollywood Tower Hotel and discover the real story behind the tragic and spooky happenings from October 31, 1939: the date when the lift mysteriously became haunted by a group of unfortunate hotel guests!

This tour is only provided in French. Buying a ticket for the tour does not mean you have access to the rides: you will need to also have a Studios ticket to be able to go on the rides from 10am when it officially opens. It costs €25 for adults (12 +),€15 for children aged 3–11 and under-3s go free.

Book before you arrive by contacting the Disney Special Activities team at **dlp.disney.special.activities@disney.com**

PARK DETAILS

OPENING HOURS	**Low Season (Autumn and Winter)** ■ Monday to Friday: 10 – 6pm ■ Saturday and Sunday: 7pm **High Season (Spring and Summer)** ■ Monday to Sunday: 10am – 9pm (11pm in school holidays) Times subject to change without notice – keep up to date through the website www.disneylandparis.co.uk

Scan the QR code for park opening times.

PARKING	Parking for Disney Hotel guests is free at both your hotel and in the Disney Car Park in front of the parks. For non-Disney Hotel visitors, parking in the Disney Car Park costs the following: ■ Cars €20 per day ■ Vehicles over 2 metres high €20 per day ■ Campervans €35 per day ■ Motorbikes €15 per day

Art of Disney Animation.

ATTRACTIONS	At-a-glance age group suitability (height restrictions have been taken into account)			
	Under 5s	5–8s	9–12s	Over 12s
Front Lot				
Studio 1	•	•	•	•
Toon Studio				
Art of Disney Animation	•	•	•	•
Mickey and the Magician	•	•	•	•
Flying Carpets Over Agrabah	•	•	•	
Crush's Coaster			•	•
Cars Quatre Roues Rallye	•	•	•	
Ratatouille: The Adventure	•	•	•	•
RC Racer			•	•
Slinky Dog ZigZag Spin	•	•	•	
Toy Soldiers Parachute Drop		•	•	
Production Courtyard				
Studio Tram Tour: Behind the Magic		•	•	
The Twilight Zone Tower of Terror				•
Disney Junior Live on Stage!	•	•		
Stitch Live!	•	•	•	•
Backlot				
Armageddon: les Effets Spéciaux			•	•
Rock 'n' Roller Coaster starring Aerosmith				•
Moteurs...Action!			•	•

8 Disney Village

Disney Village, situated just outside Walt Disney Studios and Disneyland Park, is a bright, busy mini shopping district with multiple restaurant and entertainment options available.

Scan the QR code above for an online map of Disney Village.

Designed mainly to cater to those staying in the surrounding Disney hotels, the village is free to access and is equally perfect for anyone looking for even more merchandise, shows and themed food beyond the perimeter of the Disney parks.

Restaurants

Vapiano
- €€ - *Moderately priced*
- *Quick counter service*
- *TripAdvisor: 3.5*

The German-owned restaurant chain Vapiano opened a new branch in Disney Village in July 2016. It has taking the place of the former NEX Arcade, an area of 1000 square metres, located to the right of the entrance of World of Disney. Specialising in Italian-inspired dishes of pasta and pizza, everything is homemade including the desserts, which is a real boon at Disneyland where the majority of the restaurants are quite the opposite. The 'fast casual' concept includes fresh produce cooked in front of customers, open seating at shared tables and an innovative smart card payment system. Many of the reviews rave about the quality and freshness of the food although some complain about the wait times for food service – even likening it to the wait for rides in the parks!

Five Guys Burger
- €€ - *Moderately priced*
- *Quick counter service*

Newly opened in March 2017, Five Guys Burger is right next door to Vapiano's. You can get quality American burgers here with a choice of 15 toppings to suit your own tastes. Five Guys also serves excellent hand-cut fries, hot dogs, milk shakes and a selection of drinks. Reviewers say the burgers are full of flavour and portions are generous but vegetarians say there is not much for them to choose from.

Planet Hollywood
- €€ - *Moderately priced*
- *Table Service*
- *TripAdvisor: 3.5*
- *11.30am–midnight*

Who doesn't want to climb into the centre of a giant blue planet to eat under a planetarium-style night sky in a reasonably priced restaurant? Add in a pop soundtrack, classic film memorabilia and all of your favourite film (and, of course, Disney) characters and this becomes a fun-filled dining

experience. The menu is simple and predictable, offering a selection of burgers, pasta dishes and grill specialities. With a main meal costing anywhere between €15 and €25, this is certainly not the most expensive dining experience in Disneyland Paris. In mid-afternoon, even in peak times, it's usually nice and quiet, so eat then and you'll be leaving just as the restaurant has filled up with a queue building outside. Reviewers are generally satisfied that this meets the expectations of any branch of the Planet Hollywood chain.

King Ludwig's Castle

- ■ *€€ - Moderately priced*
- ■ *Table Service*
- ■ *Reservation available*
- ■ *TripAdvisor: 3.5*
- ■ *11.30am–11pm (Sun–Thur) 11.30am–midnight (Fri and Sat)*

Around the corner from Planet Hollywood is King Ludwig's Castle: a dining experience themed on a grand Bavarian dining hall. Set menus of semi-traditional German cuisine (arguably more international than German) place you between €20 and €25 per person: you can easily eat like a king without an excessive price tag. They even have German ales available for anyone craving a taste of something not Hollywood-themed, although the TripAdvisor reviews seem to vary drastically: many reviews comment that slow service is a major issue while others admire the warm, wood-panelled interior and royal detailing. King Ludwig's Castle also has a Boutique attached to it with an array of souvenirs, many on a medieval theme.

King Ludwig's Castle

Book your table at King Ludwig's Castle through the Dining Reservation Service on +33 1 60 30 40 50 or at the reception desk at your Disney Hotel.

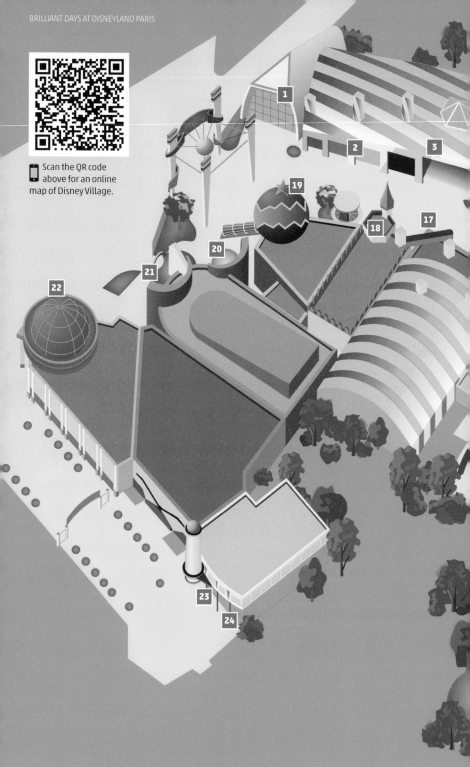

Scan the QR code above for an online map of Disney Village.

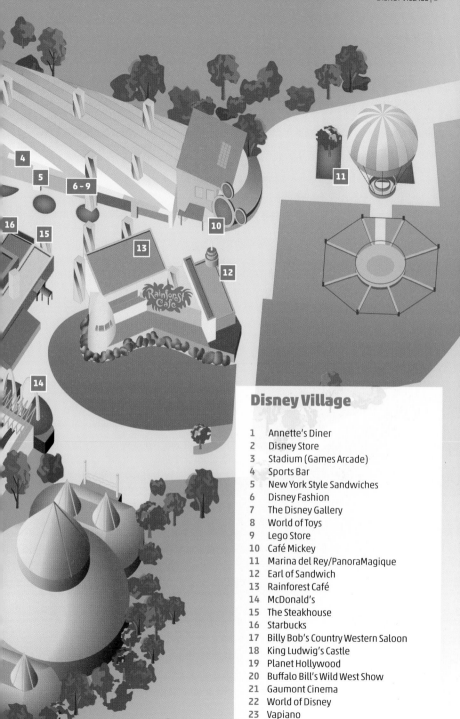

Disney Village

1 Annette's Diner
2 Disney Store
3 Stadium (Games Arcade)
4 Sports Bar
5 New York Style Sandwiches
6 Disney Fashion
7 The Disney Gallery
8 World of Toys
9 Lego Store
10 Café Mickey
11 Marina del Rey/PanoraMagique
12 Earl of Sandwich
13 Rainforest Café
14 McDonald's
15 The Steakhouse
16 Starbucks
17 Billy Bob's Country Western Saloon
18 King Ludwig's Castle
19 Planet Hollywood
20 Buffalo Bill's Wild West Show
21 Gaumont Cinema
22 World of Disney
23 Vapiano
24 Five Guys

Annette's Diner

Annette's Diner
- ■ *€€ - Moderately priced*
- ■ *Table Service*
- ■ *Trip Advisor: 3.5*
- ■ *10am–midnight*

Across the main walkway through the Disney Village is an alternative dining experience to the medium-priced sit down dinner options we have shown so far. Here you can find Annette's Diner, unsurprisingly offering even more American cuisine but this time with an authentic 1950s Americana backdrop.

Set menus cost you anywhere between €20 and €35 per head, so this is not the cheapest eatery in the Disney Village, but who can fail to enjoy a diner that has all the waiting staff on roller-skates and a jukebox belting out the old favourite tunes. TripAdvisor reviews mostly agree that this is value for money, with many praising the 'good food and service' and the short wait. One or two have been disappointed that the '50s theming (roller-skates for example) have not been in evidence on their visit.

Sports Bar
- ■ *€ - Low prices*
- ■ *Bar*
- ■ *TripAdvisor: 3*
- ■ *2pm–1am Mon–Fri, midday–2am Sat, midday–1am Sun*

This is the ideal location for sports fans who want to catch the live action on a giant screen while enjoying a pint or two. The bar serves draught beers such as Kronenberg, Fosters and Carlsberg as well as a good selection of bottled beers. You can also enjoy a simple, tasty snack and a set meal of hot dog and fries plus a brownie and a soft drink will cost you around €12. Popular with tourists and locals alike it can be a lively place to come most evenings and in the summer months you can make the most of the outdoor terrace.

New York Style Sandwiches

New York Style Sandwiches
- ■ *€ - low prices*
- ■ *Quick counter service*
- ■ *TripAdvisor: 2*
- ■ *9am–midnight Mon– Thurs, 9am –11pm Fri and Sat, 9am– midnight Sun*

Styling itself as a Manhattan sandwich deli, reviews seem to suggest that this particular eatery hasn't quite hit the mark. Guests have remarked on the sandwiches being 'dry and

tasteless' with 'terrible food and service', although many have mentioned that it works as a quick fix or in providing a broad selection for vegetarians. You are looking at around €8 per sandwich, while a set menu costs around €15 per person, including a main course, side, dessert and drink. As always, even if the food isn't quite what you were looking for, the Broadway memorabilia and mirrored walls at least set the scene.

Billy Bob's Country Western Saloon
- ■ *€ - low prices*
- ■ *Quick counter service*
- ■ *TripAdvisor: 2*
- ■ *6pm–1am Sun–Fri, 6pm –2am Sat with snacks served from 6–10.30pm*

Billy Bob's Country Western Saloon

Themed on the Wild West, you can have a drink in the Saloon-style bar at Billy Bob's with some bar snacks and Tex-Mex bites such as nachos, spare ribs and chicken nuggets costing less than €15 per person. However, it's the music concerts that are the big draw for guests at Billy Bob's, which provide a musical treat for kids and adults alike. Whether you have a penchant for rock, jazz, blues or pop, there's a little something for everyone, although you will have to check at the venue for a programme of its upcoming events.

For a more modern sound, Billy Bob's Saloon also plays host to the Music Party, bringing together a selection of DJs to pump out some of the latest tunes. Some might find this a little jarring with the Texan surroundings, but it promises a night of fun for any teenagers or young adults in your family.

Keep your eye open for various musically themed weekends at Billy Bob's Saloon. One of the more popular events is the Blues weekend, bringing the sounds of the Deep South – with saxophone solos, and harmonica harmonies – to this little corner of the Disney Village.

La Grange Restaurant
- ■ *€€€ - High prices*
- ■ *Buffet*
- ■ *Reservations accepted*
- ■ *TripAdvisor: 3.5*
- ■ *6–11pm daily*

For a more thorough selection of Tex Mex food, head upstairs to the La Grange Restaurant at Billy Bob's Country Western Saloon. Here you can enjoy a varied buffet that includes barbecue ribs, chicken wings, chilli con carne, salad, cornbread and more. Adults pay around €30 per head, with children at around €15 (aged 3 to 11).

Reservations can be made through the usual Dining Reservation Service on **+33 1 60 30 40 50** or at the reception desk of your Disney hotel.

Starbucks Coffee

- *€ - Low prices*
- *Quick counter service*
- *8am–midnight Sun–Thur, 8am–11pm Fri and Sat*

Starbucks

Heralding itself as an eco-friendly, sustainable coffee house, Starbucks in Disney Village offers all of your favourite coffee flavours and tasty snacks but with an eco-friendly twist. If you're moving from one park to the other during the mid-afternoon, this is an ideal place to come for that pick-me-up in between rides.

The Steakhouse

- *€€€ - High prices*
- *Table Service*
- *Reservations*
- *TripAdvisor: 3.5*
- *Noon–midnight daily*

This may be another American-themed restaurant, but they've moved away from the Wild West and into 1950s Chicago. As the name suggests, The Steakhouse provides various cuts of tender steak with a variety of sides, with set menus ranging between €30 and €60 per head. Reviews on TripAdvisor mostly point to the excellence of the food but suggest that the prices are a bit high – some of the highest in Disney Village. Book a table through the Dining Reservation Service on +33 1 60 30 40 50 or at the reception desk of your Disney Hotel.

Café Mickey

- *€€€ - High prices*
- *Table Service*
- *Reservations available*
- *Trip Advisor: 3.5*
- *7.30am–11pm Sun–Fri, 7.30am–midnight Sat*

Café Mickey

Once a popular venue for a meal with the Mickey and plenty more Disney characters, Café Mickey is now a simple Italian-American diner. The character appearances have moved to the **Plaza Gardens Restaurant** in Main Street, Disneyland Park for breakfast only. The prices here were always steep for the quality of the food on offer, and many reviewers feel that the design and décor of the place is also very tired. Many more also report less than satisfactory food and also some service issues. Without the lure of the characters, it is questionable whether this restaurant will survive in its current guise; so do not be surprised to find it closed for renovation at some point. The restaurant offers a standard set menu of two or three courses starting at €35 per head, although this may be reviewed now that the characters are no longer in attendance. You can book a table before you arrive through the Dining Reservation Service on **+33 1 60 30 40 50** or at the desk of your Disney hotel.

Rainforest Café

Rainforest Café

- *€€ - Moderately priced*
- *Table service*
- *TripAdvisor: 3.5*
- *11.30am–midnight daily*

Feel at home in a tropical setting by trying out the surprisingly American menu available at the Rainforest Café. Burgers, pasta dishes and roasted chicken form just a part of the standard menu that will set you back anything between €15 and €25 per head, while the jungle sounds, colourful foliage and waterfalls take you away from France and into a whole other world.

Just in case you feel like picking up some jungle-themed memorabilia while you are there, a friendly boutique is to hand, with all of the costumes and plush toys a budding adventurer could dream of.

Earl of Sandwich

Earl of Sandwich
- ■ *€ - Low prices*
- ■ *Quick counter service*
- ■ *TripAdvisor: 4*
- ■ *10am–11pm*

Next door to the Rainforest Café you can pick up a quick sandwich for around €8 from the Earl of Sandwich eatery. The décor is based on the library of the fourth Earl of Sandwich and overlooks Lake Disney. Reviews state that this particular fast food joint provides 'the best value for money' throughout the Village, while managing to supply 'sensational' sandwiches.

McDonald's
- ■ *€ - Low prices*
- ■ *Quick Counter service*
- ■ *TripAdvisor: 3*
- ■ *8am–midnight Sun–Thur, 8am–1am Fri and Sat*

This modern version of the familiar chain serves all the usual fast foods, although you won't necessarily save much time here as queues can be long and the service is slow. It is particularly popular in the evening as it is one of the cheaper options in Disney Village.

World of Disney Store

Shops

World of Disney
It seems that only one Disney store really holds a bit of everything, and that is the World of Disney! Situated at the entrance to the Disney Village, this is the largest shop in the whole of Disneyland Paris, and offers some unique souvenirs.

Disney Store
Pass under the neon blue lights to find even more souvenirs based on your favourite films and Disney characters – if you haven't maxed out your credit card already!

Disney Fashion
Take your pick from a variety of printed T-shirts, accessories and varied designs at this store – for all sizes and ages!

The Disney Gallery
Next door from Disney Fashion, you can find yet another Disney store, this time focusing on the art behind the magic. Get your hands on limited edition prints, models and posters, and even get your chosen item delivered to your home address for ease of transport.

World of Toys
Collectible prints may be a little too grown-up for certain members of your family, so thankfully there is a toy shop perfectly placed one door up to help fulfil your child's wish list. Find the perfect costume, toy or accessory for the princesses, fairies, pirates or spacemen in your family.

World of Toys

The Lego Store
Disney meets the creative world of Lego in this store, displaying all of the individual figures and themed sets available for you to take home and construct.

Entertainment

Gaumont and IMAX Cinema Complex
With 15 massive screens showing some of the biggest blockbusters of the moment, the Gaumont Cinema Complex uses the latest sound technology to bring you that little bit closer to the action. Obviously most of the films are in French, with only one or two shown in their original language so if you do not speak French you will have to strike it lucky to find something suitable. Those in French are labelled VF, those in their original language without subtitles VO and those in the original language with subtitles VOST. Scan the QR code to visit the Gaumont Cinema website for more details and the film schedule.

Scan the QR code above for the Gaumont Cinema website.

Tickets place you at around €5 for children under 14, and around €11 to €12 for adults for regular showings.

Buffalo Bill's Wild West Show
- ■ *€€€ - High prices*
- ■ *Table Service*
- ■ *Reservation available*
- ■ *TripAdvisor: 4.5*
- ■ *Show times: 6.30pm and 9.30pm, guests can arrive up to 45mins beforehand.*

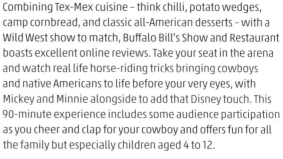

Buffalo Bill's Wild West Show.

Combining Tex-Mex cuisine – think chilli, potato wedges, camp cornbread, and classic all-American desserts – with a Wild West show to match, Buffalo Bill's Show and Restaurant boasts excellent online reviews. Take your seat in the arena and watch real life horse-riding tricks bringing cowboys and native Americans to life before your very eyes, with Mickey and Minnie alongside to add that Disney touch. This 90-minute experience includes some audience participation as you cheer and clap for your cowboy and offers fun for all the family but especially children aged 4 to 12.

Tickets are priced differently according to the seating. 1st category seating has the best views and costs €76.90 (£58.65) for adults and €61.90 (£47.21) for children. 2nd category costs €61.90 (£47.21) for adults and €46.90 (£35.77) for children.

TripAdvisor reviews all seem to be outstandingly positive, branding the experience as an 'awesome evening', a 'fantastic last night in Disney' and – to put it simply 'Yeehaaa Cowboy'!

The popularity of this particular experience makes reservations essential – so don't forget to book your Wild West evening through the Dining Reservation Service on + 33 1 60 45 71 00, or at the reception desk of your Disney Hotel.

PanoraMagique
- *1st April to 31st Oct: every day from 9am–11pm*
- *1st Nov to 31st Mar: every day from 10am–8pm*

PanoraMagique.

Transporting up to 30 guests at a time, Disney claim that 'PanoraMagique is one of the biggest hot air balloon rides in the world'. The tethered balloon takes off and lands from its own purpose-built platform on Lake Disney. The ride lasts about six minutes offering panoramic views of the surrounding parks and region of France and some great photo opportunities. It costs €12 for adults (aged 12+): €6 for children 3 to 11 and is free for under-3s.

Flights will not take place if there are high winds or adverse weather conditions so it is advisable to check on the day of your visit by phoning +33 (0)1 60 45 70 52.

Indoor games consoles
The Stadium provides an indoor interactive activities area to keep your family occupied if the weather doesn't hold out. The games consoles range from arcade classics to driving simulators to dance machines, supplying you with entertainment as long as you have a pocket of change and a bit of time to spare.

Events

Here is a rundown of the various events that occur in and around the Disney Village all year long. These events are subject to change, so check the website before your trip.

Spring

St David's Welsh Festival

Celebrate all things Welsh with Minnie and Mickey at the St David's Welsh festival in the Disney Village. Held over the closest weekend to 1 March, Welsh food, drink and dance are all on offer, as well as traditional costumes, a fireworks display and face painting for the kids.

St Patrick's Day Festival

On St Patrick's Day (March 17) the Disney Village seizes the chance to embrace the vibrant emerald colours of Irish heritage, along with the traditional Celtic music, dancing and costumes. Something for everyone in the family, including the usual face painting for the kids and an impressive closing firework display.

Country and Western Jamboree

If both Billy Bob's and Buffalo Bill's don't offer enough Country and Western entertainment to suit your needs, then you might want to visit Disneyland Paris in April for the Country and Western Jamboree in Disney Village. This festival promises cavalry parades through the streets and Country-style song and dance shows to give you that American Frontier feel.

Jazz Fest

From the Blues weekend at Billy Bob's to the Village's Jazz Fest, there is a musical moment to suit all tastes! Usually taking place in April, straight after the end of the Country Jamboree, jazz musicians from all over Europe come to this two-day festival to showcase some incredible musical talent right on the Disneyland doorstep.

Summer

Brazilian Rhythm

Summer sees the Village take on a Latino vibe by embracing the carnival spirit. The streets are filled with music, dancing and the bright colours of Brazil, with night-time carnivals and special shows providing Salsa and Samba demonstrations.

Scan the QR code above for more information on events happening in the Disney Village

Scan the QR code above to download the Disney Village programme.

Autumn

Rock'n'Roll Festival

This three-day event in early September brings 1950s-style rock 'n' roll to the concerts and entertainment venues of the Disney Village, while you can equally check out the gorgeous collection of vintage motors on show at the 'drive-in'.

Halloween at Disney Village

Halloween runs throughout October and sees Disney Village transformed into a spooky scene of horror, complete with a parade of pumpkins and various well-known characters sporting special costumes. On October 31st the village is overrun with Halloween street entertainment and special spooky concerts and shows.

Mickey's Magical Fireworks and Bonfire

While most big Disney events end with a spectacular fireworks display, sometimes Mickey pulls out all the stops with a bonfire and spectacular music on the shores of Lake Disney for three separate nights in early November.

Winter

Christmas and New Year at Disney Village

If you are thinking of travelling to Disneyland Paris around the Christmas and New Year period, take a stroll through the Disney Village to check out the celebrations and festivities on offer amidst the glowing fairy lights and the delicate sprinkling of decorative snow. The various eateries and venues will be offering festive menus and special shows for your family's entertainment – although expect this period to be both busier and a little more on the pricey side.

Disney Village Web Radio

And even when you find yourself in another part of the world, far away from the Disney Village or even Disneyland Paris, you can tune into the Disney Village Radio channel online. Listen to the playlists of various Village restaurants – such as the Disney classics to be heard at Café Mickey's or the Country Rock found at Billy Bob's – or check out the Club Mix over the weekends. There are also shows to check out and the latest updates from the magical world of Disneyland Paris.

Outside Disneyland Paris

9

When the magic of Disney becomes a bit overwhelming, exploring other attractions and entertainment outside the parks can be a welcome relief. Whether you're an avid golfer or just wanting to wander the streets of Paris for a day, here are a few options to give your Disneyland trip that much needed variation.

Excursions to Paris

With the City of Lights only a 45-minute train ride away, Paris provides the perfect cultural day-trip for all ages. Here are two of the package day tour options that Disney offer to keep you and your family occupied.

Magical Day Tour

- Adults: £93
- Kids (3–11): £66

Includes:
- Coach trip to and from the centre of Paris
- Coach city tour with individual headsets
- River cruise along the Seine with individual audio guides
- Visit to the Louvre Museum (90 mins approx) OR Visit to the second floor of the Eiffel Tower

Departing from and returning to: Disney's Hotel New York

When: Every day (except certain days of the year, check the website)

Time leaves: 9:45am

Returns: 6:30pm (traffic depending)

Other aspects of this trip you will need to consider:
- Lunch is not included
- You must choose either the Eiffel Tower or the Louvre Museum when you book the excursion

Scan the QR code above to book the Magical Day Tour online.

- There are special audios designed for children available too
- Even if you choose the Louvre option, you will still be able to see the Eiffel Tower as it is right next to the departure/return point of the Seine Cruise, but you will not be able to go up it

Scan the QR code to check when and how to book online.

Paris Essentials Tour

- **Adults**: £60
- **Kids** (3–11): £42

Includes:

- Coach trip to and from the centre of Paris
- A hop-on, hop-off city tour on an open-top double-decker bus with individual headsets – this tour takes you past many of the major Parisian landmarks such as Notre-Dame Cathedral, the Eiffel Tower, up the Champs-Elysées and past the Opera House (the Palais Garnier)
- Lots of free time to explore the city how you like

Departing from and returning to: Disney's Newport Bay Club, Vienna International Magic Circus Hotel and Hôtel L'Elysée Val d'Europe

When: Every day (except certain days of the year, check the website)

Time leaves: 10:00am

Returns: 7:00pm (traffic depending)

Other aspects of this trip you will need to consider:

- Lunch is not included

Scan the QR code to check when and how to book.

Scan the QR code above to book the Paris Essentials Tour online.

Planning your own trip to Paris

With Marne-la-Vallee/Chessy RER station right outside the parks it couldn't be easier to get to the centre of Paris. An organised tour is great if it's your choice, but it's far from essential. If you prefer to take your own trip into the centre of Paris, here are a few things to keep in mind:

- RER A Trains into the centre of the city take around 45 minutes from Marne-la-Vallée/Chessy.
- Individual metro tickets, books of 10 or 20 tickets or passes can be bought from stations either at the automated machines or the manned kiosks.
- If you plan to visit several sights in the city and will be on and off the Metro all day, consider the Mobilis card which gives you all day unlimited travel across up to five Zones. Marne-la-Vallee/Chessy is in Zone 5.

Eiffel Tower.

- Scan the QR code to find metro map. If you're in a Disney hotel, make use of the concierge. They will advise you on which type of train ticket to buy; if you tell them you want to get somewhere specific such as, for example, the Eiffel Tower or Bateaux Mouches, they will give you a free map and advise you on the route and the closest Metro stop.
- If you want to visit a number of museums or galleries, it might be worth your while investing in a Museum Pass. Scan the QR code to find out more about this option.

Scan the QR code above to find a Paris metro map.

Shopping

Val d'Europe is one of the biggest shopping centres in Europe with around 130 stores, restaurants and cafes as well as the SeaLife Aquarium. The Auchen hypermarket here is a good place to stock up on food and wine at reasonable prices. It is open from 8.30am to 10pm, independent of the rest of the mall.

The outlet-shopping village La Vallée is right next door to Val d'Europe with all items discounted by at least 33 per cent. Simply take one stop by train from Marne-la-Vallee/Chessy train station (€1.90 per journey) and follow signs for 'Centre Commercial' when you arrive. You can also catch the number 50 bus for free which leaves from outside the train station.

Scan the QR code above for more information about a Museum Pass.

SeaLife Aquarium.

SeaLife Aquarium
- **Open every day** (Closed on December 25th and morning of January 1st)
- **Hours:**
  Sunday–Friday: 10:00am – 6:30pm (last admission at 5:30 pm)
  Saturday: 10:00am – 9:00pm (last admission at 8:00 pm)

Scan the QR code above for more information and book your tickets for the SeaLife Aquarium.

The SeaLife Aquarium in Val d'Europe holds around 50 tanks with more than 350 different species to see and to learn about, from all corners of the blue planet. You and your family can get even closer to these unique tropical creatures with a 360° underwater tunnel bringing you up close and personal with some fearsome sharks. There are also various educational talks, touch pools and feeding sessions available throughout the week.

Save money by booking your trip to SeaLife in advance. Scan the QR cor more information and to buy your tickets.

Golf

Disney Golf Course

Situated right next to both the Radisson Blu Hotel and the Marriott's Village Ile de France accommodation, the Disney Golf Course is only a 10-minute drive from the parks.

Scan the QR code above for more information on courses or lessons at the Disney Golf Course.

- Open 7 days per week
- Three 9-hole courses combine to make various 18-hole rounds
- Individual private lessons are available
- Group sessions are also available

Scan the QR code for more information on courses or lessons, or call +33 1 60 45 68 90.

Scan the QR code for general prices for green fees.

Scan the QR code above for general prices and green fees at the Disney Golf Course.

Take a break from the game by trying out either The Club House bar and restaurant or the Club House Grill. Both provide food and drink options at a moderate price whilst you look out over the rolling greens of the surrounding course.

The Bussy-Guermantes Course

Perfectly placed if you are planning to stay at the Best Western Golf Hotel, the Bussy-Guermantes Course offers both 9- and 18-hole course options for a variety of abilities. Their prices are as follows:

Scan the QR code to find out more information about this golf course through their website.

Scan the QR code above for more information on the Bussy-Guermantes Golf Course.

Practical information

Baby Care Centres

These are located next door to Plaza Gardens Restaurant, at the top of Main Street on the right at Disneyland Park and behind the Studio Services in Front Lot, just inside the entrance on the right. Here you will find baby changing facilities as well as a feeding room with baby food available to buy. Most toilets also have baby changing facilities.

Baby sitting

Guests of Disney Hotels can take advantage of their Baby Sitting Service. Please enquire at the reception desk of your Disney Hotel.

Clothing and footwear

You will spend a lot of time on your feet at the parks so comfortable footwear such as trainers is essential. For safety reasons children must not wear shoes with wheels in them. Casual wear such as shorts and T-shirts are acceptable at the parks and in most restaurants. A shirt/top and shoes must be worn at all times in the parks.

Disabled guests

Disneyland Paris is designed to cater for all guests whatever their physical or mental capabilities. Wheelchair rental, disabled parking, adapted minibuses for transfer from Disney hotels, guidebooks in Braille and induction loops are just a few examples of services on offer.

On arrival at the parks disabled guests should go to City Hall (Disneyland Park) or Studio Services (Walt Disney Studios) where a cast member will give them information on which rides are most easily accessible according to their disability and will issue a priority card, if necessary. The priority card allows a permanently disabled guest (along with up to four members of their party) access to a ride via a specially adapted entrance. To get a priority card you will need to present your disability card or a medical certificate.

Guests with a temporary disability and pregnant mothers can apply for an Easy Access Card which works in a similar way to the priority card. They will need to present a medical certificate signed and stamped by a doctor.

For more information read the Disney Parks Accessibility Guide on the Disneyland Paris website.

Wheelchair rental

You can rent a wheelchair for the day for €20 from either park, but you will need to put down a deposit of €75. Wheelchair rental is located to the right of the main entrance just under the railway arch for Disneyland Park and on the right hand side of the entrance courtyard to the left of Studio Photo for Walt Disney Studios.

Emergency details

- Police 17 or 112
- Fire brigade 18 or 112
- 24-hour doctor 01 47 07 77 77
- 24-hour medical emergencies 15 or 112
- Less serious medical incidents 18 or 112
- Public ambulance service 01 45 13 67 89

British Embassy, Paris

- 35, rue du Faubourg, St Honore, 75363 Paris Cedex 08 Paris
- Mon-Fri: 9.30am to 1pm, 2.30pm to 6pm
- Tel: (33) 1 44 51 31 00

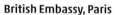 Scan the QR code above for the website of the British Embassy in Paris.

First Aid

First aid rooms can be found next to the Baby Care Centres in both parks and help is also available at Disney Hotels and Disney Village. Trained staff are available to assist with any medical needs you might have and can administer plasters, paracetamol and basic first aid.

Internet access and Wi-Fi

There is no wireless internet in the parks themselves but Disney Village offers a number of locations with good free Wi-Fi: Sports Bar, Billy Bob's Country Western Saloon, The Steakhouse, Buffalo Bill's Wild West Show, Earl of Sandwich, McDonald's and Starbucks. Wi-Fi is available at all the Disney hotels and partner hotels.

Lockers

For a small fee you can store any items (including picnics) at the Guest Storage facility located to the right of Main Street, close to the Disneyland Hotel. Bulky items such as suitcases should be left here as they are not allowed in the parks. After entering the park through the ticket barriers, take the exit

FRENCH PHRASES

English	French
Good morning/Hello	Bonjour
Good evening	Bonsoir
Goodbye	Au revoir
Do you speak English?	Parlez-vous anglais?
I don't understand	Je ne comprends pas
Please	S'il vous plait
Thank you	Merci
Could you speak slowly please?	Pouvez vous parlez plus lentement, s'il vous plait?
Yes	Oui
No	Non
I would like...	Je voudrais...
Do you have...?	Avez-vous...?
How much is that?	Combien ça coûte?
The bill, please	L'addition, s'il vous plait
Coffee	Café
White coffee	Café au lait
Tea	Thé
Where are the toilets?	Où sont les toilettes?
Can you take a photo of us please?	Pouvez-vous prendre une photo de nous, s'il vous plais?
Toll road	Route à péage
Toll booths	Les péages
Motorway service areas	Aires
Shopping centre	Le centre commercial

for the Disneyland Hotel making sure you get your hand stamped for re-entry to the parks. You can access it as often as you need to during the day.

Lost children

If you lose your child during your time at the parks, let a Cast Member know immediately. Calls are put out across the park and when your child is found they will be taken to the appropriate Baby Care Centre ready to be reunited with family.

Scan the QR code above for the website of the Hertford British Hospital.

Scan the QR code above for the website of the American Hospital of Paris.

Lost property

If you lose (or find) any personal items at the parks, head for the Lost and Found locations: City Hall in the Disneyland Park or Studio Services at Walt Disney Studios Park. If you only discover you've lost something when you get home, contact Disneyland Paris directly.

Medical matters

Most hospitals will have staff who speak some English but there are two fully English-speaking hospitals in Paris:

- the **Hertford British Hospital**, 3 Rue Barbès, 92300 Levallois-Perret; 01 46 39 22 22; (scan the QR code for its website) and
- the **American Hospital of Paris**; 63, Boulevard Victor Hugo 92200 Neuilly-sur-Seine; 01 46 41 25 25 (scan the QR code for its website)

The nearest pharmacy to the parks can be found at Val d'Europe Shopping Centre close to the train station. It is open Mon–Sat 10am–9pm.

Money

The French currency is the Euro, and obviously if you're taking cash you should get this before you leave home as airports, train stations and Disney hotels offer the worst exchange rates. Generally, it's only necessary to carry a small amount of cash with you, as there are plenty of cash dispensers around the resort. Credit cards, master cards, Maestro and Visa are widely accepted in most restaurants, bars and shops. Be aware, though, that most banks add additional fees when paying by card in a foreign currency. Remember to inform your bank that you will be visiting France so that they don't put a block on your card in the mistaken assumption that it's been stolen.

An even better option is to get a pre-paid debit card such as the FairFX card (available in the UK only). You can use this to make any purchases with no additional fees and you can top it up as you go. The exchange rates are good and are fixed on loading. There is however a charge of £9.95 for the card. The current exchange rate is £1 = €1.13 or €1 = 0.89 pence which means something costing €10 is equivalent to just under £8.90, approximately.

Park Entertainment Schedule

As you enter the parks, along by the paper maps in several different languages, are the daily entertainment schedules which give you all the character meet-and-greets, parades and shows happening that day in the park, where and at what time.

Parking

The Disney car park is well signed and is located at the front of the parks. Cars cost €20 per day; vehicles over 2 metres high €20; campervans €35 and motorbikes €15.

Passports

All members of your family will need a full, valid passport that will not expire for three months after you enter France. Non-British subjects should check their visa requirements in advance. For UK passport enquiries, call the UK government's passport adviceline on **0300 222 0000** or scan the QR code for the UK government's passport advice webpage.

Scan the QR code above for the UK goverment's passport advice webpage.

Phone calls

If you think you will need to phone the UK a number of times on your trip it's worth checking what your mobile phone provider will charge for calls from abroad and see if there are better plans available to you. Otherwise you can buy phone cards and use public payphones when you are there. Avoid using hotel phones if at all possible as they are extremely expensive. To call the UK from France, dial 00 44 and then the UK number, omitting the first 0 from the area code.

Picnics

Despite what some guidebooks might say, you are allowed to bring your own food and drink into the parks. You aren't allowed to sit on the lawns to eat it but there are plenty of benches scattered throughout the parks. A rucksack filled with such items as sandwiches, fruit, snacks, water and other drinks is fine as long as you don't have alcoholic beverages or anything in glass containers (apart from baby food). Group picnics that require specific equipment such as cool boxes, tables and containers are only allowed to take place in the designated picnic area to the side of the entrance walkway from the main parking lot.

Pushchair (stroller) rental

Even if your child doesn't use their pushchair (stroller) at home it's a good idea to hire one in Disneyland Paris. A full day in the park is really a lot of walking, even for adults. You can rent a pushchair (stroller) for the day for a fee from either park, and you will need to put down a deposit if you want to take them out of the parks, move between parks or enter Disney Village. Pushchair (stroller) rental is located to the right of the main entrance just under the railway arch for Disneyland Park and on the right hand side of the entrance courtyard to the left of Studio Photo for Walt Disney Studios.

Restaurants

There are a number of different types of restaurant available at Disneyland Paris. Buffet restaurants have a selection of food available at the buffet bar. You can go up as many times as you want and eat as much as you like. Some buffet meals also include drinks, but it depends on the restaurant. Character buffets include characters to interact with. Counter service or quick service venues operate in the same way as McDonalds but are often slow due to long queues and poor service. At able or sit down service restaurants you select from the menu at your table and a waiter or waitress comes to take your order.

Restaurant reservations

If there is a specific restaurant you would like to eat at it is worth booking in advance. Restaurants take bookings up to 60 days in advance but you will usually be able to get a table two weeks in advance. To make a reservation phone +33 (0) 1 60 30 40 50 (they speak English). You can also book at any Disney hotel lobby, at City Hall in Disneyland Park or at Studio Services at Walt Disney Studios.

Security

Security checkpoints are located at the entrance to Disneyland Park and Walt Disney Studios. Security personnel will quickly check every bag for prohibited items which include wheeled items (including large suitcases), alcoholic beverages, weapons, folding chairs, glass containers and pets other than service animals and guide dogs.

Shopping

If you purchase something from a resort shop, you don't have to carry it around with you all day. Disney offers a free service whereby you can leave your purchases in the store and pick them up again as you leave the parks, or at Disney Village after 6pm or at the boutique in your Disney Hotel after 8pm. Apart from the shops around the resort, there are also two shopping centres of note, just a short ride on the RER: Val d'Europe and La Vallée.

Smoking

Despite what the Disneyland Paris website says, people smoke in every outdoor area at the parks and in the ride queues. It's really noticeable compared to UK theme parks, but that's just how it is.

Time difference

France is one hour ahead of the UK. It's a good idea to change your watch en route or as soon as you arrive so you don't get important timings wrong at the parks.

Tipping

It is the law in France for restaurants to include a 15% service charge. This is always included in the price on the menu and will either be itemised on your bill or the words 'service compris' will indicate that the service charge has already been included in the total to be paid. You are therefore not obliged to add a tip in cafes or restaurants but if you want to say thank you to an individual for good service a rough guide is 5 to 10%.

A good tip for hotel porters is €1 per bag, a hotel maid or doorman €1 to €2 and taxi drivers 5–10% of the fare.

Tourist information

Maps, advice and information on any local sights and attractions can be found at any Offices de Tourisme. The closest to the parks is at Place François Truffaut 77705 Marne-la-Vallée or if you are in central Paris there is one at Les Galeries Lafayette, 40 Boulevard Haussman 75009.

Toilets (restrooms)

These are located throughout the parks and shown on the park map. At the park entrance, pick up a map to keep handy in your pocket for quick reference.

Travel Insurance

Make sure you have adequate travel insurance for your trip that covers such things as medical treatment, personal liability, cancellation or curtailment and personal property. Take out your travel insurance as soon as you have booked in case something happens to prevent you going on the holiday. It's worth checking if your bank or home insurance company already covers you as some provide this as part of their services. Choose a reputable company such as M&S Bank, LV, Churchill, Direct Line, Holidaysafe, Aviva or the Post Office.

Useful contact numbers/email addresses

- Annual Passport Hotline: **01 60 30 60 69**
- Billy Bob's Buffet: **01 60 30 40 50**
- Buffalo Bill's Wild West Show: **01 60 45 71 00**
- Café Mickey: **01 60 30 40 50**
- Davy Crockett's Adventure: **09 71 28 50 90**
- Disney's Davy Crockett Ranch: **01 60 45 69 00**
- Disneyland Hotel: **01 60 45 65 00**

- Disney Village: **01 60 30 20 20**
- Euro Disney SCA, Shareholders Info & Club: **01 64 74 56 30,** dlp.actionnaires@disney.com
- France Tourist Office, London: **0906 824 4123** (60p/min), info.uk@franceguide.com
- Golf Disneyland: **01 60 45 68 90**
- Hotel Cheyenne: **01 60 45 62 00**
- Hotel New York: **01 60 45 73 00**
- Hotel Santa Fe: **01 825 30 05 00**
- King Ludwig's Castle: **01 60 42 71 80**
- Lost and Found: **01 64 74 25 00**
- Mail Order Service: **01 64 74 48 48,** dlp.mail.order@disney.com
- Newport Bay Club Hotel: **01 60 45 55 00**
- Panoramagique: **01 60 45 70 52**
- Planet Hollywood: **01 60 43 78 27**
- Rainforest Café: **01 60 43 65 65**
- Resort Guest Relations: **01 60 30 60 53,** dlp.guest.communication.@disney.com
- Resort Restaurant Reservations (up to 2 months in advance): **01 60 30 40 50**
- Sea Life Aquarium: **01 60 42 33 66**
- Seine-et-Marne Tourist Office: **01 60 39 60 39,** c dt@tourisme77.fr
- Sequoia Lodge Hotel: **01 60 45 52 48**
- The Steakhouse: **01 60 30 40 50**
- UK bookings (to book a Disneyland Resort Paris stay from the UK): **08448 008 111**
- VEA Airport Shuttle Bus: **01 53 48 39 53**
- VIP Guided Tours: **01 64 74 21 26**

Write to Disneyland Paris Guest Relations: Disneyland Paris, Communication Visiteurs, BP 100, 77777, Marne-la-Vallée, Cedex 4, France

Useful websites
- http://www.disneylandparis.co.uk/
- http://www.dlptoday.com/
- http://www.dlpguide.com/
- http://www.tripadvisor.com/
- http://www.ebookers.com/
- http://www.dlpfoodguide.com/resorts.html
- http://www.attraction-tickets-direct.co.uk

Index